# Reggie Burrows Hodges

# Reggie Burrows Hodges
# Authorities of Reason

Karma

# Davide Gasparotto &
# Reggie Burrows Hodges

DAVIDE GASPAROTTO: *Authorities of Reason* is a body of work produced over the course of an extensive trip in Europe. This tour evokes the tradition of artists of the past visiting the great European capitals and ending up in Italy. What did this mean to you at this stage of your life and career?

REGGIE BURROWS HODGES: It's a trip that for most of my life would have been unimaginable. As an artist, having a chance to confront works that I had only read about taught me so much. It changed my hand. It also changed the way that I thought about how some of these works were made—as a painter, the old masters are these mystical figures, but being able to see their hand up close humanized them for me.

DG: You visited many European capitals: Amsterdam, Berlin, Copenhagen, Florence, London, Milan, Paris, Turin, and Venice. But this trip was not just about an encounter with places, it was also an encounter with paintings. In Berlin at the Gemäldegalerie you saw Titian's self-portrait when he was elderly [*Self-portrait*, c. 1550–55], and in Paris at the Louvre, the frontal, very moving self-portrait of Tintoretto when he was in his seventies [*Self-portrait*, c. 1588]. Can you talk a little bit about how the days were structured and the impact of these visits to museums?

RBH: My main priority was to see as much art as possible—

DG: And then you would go back to your hotel and just start painting? In *Golden Triangle (Paris)* (2023), we can see you working on a canvas in one of your hotel rooms.

RBH: Yes. I wanted to keep the practice close to me. I paint unstretched, which gives me a lot of flexibility to roll up the canvas and continue to move. I tried to gesso as

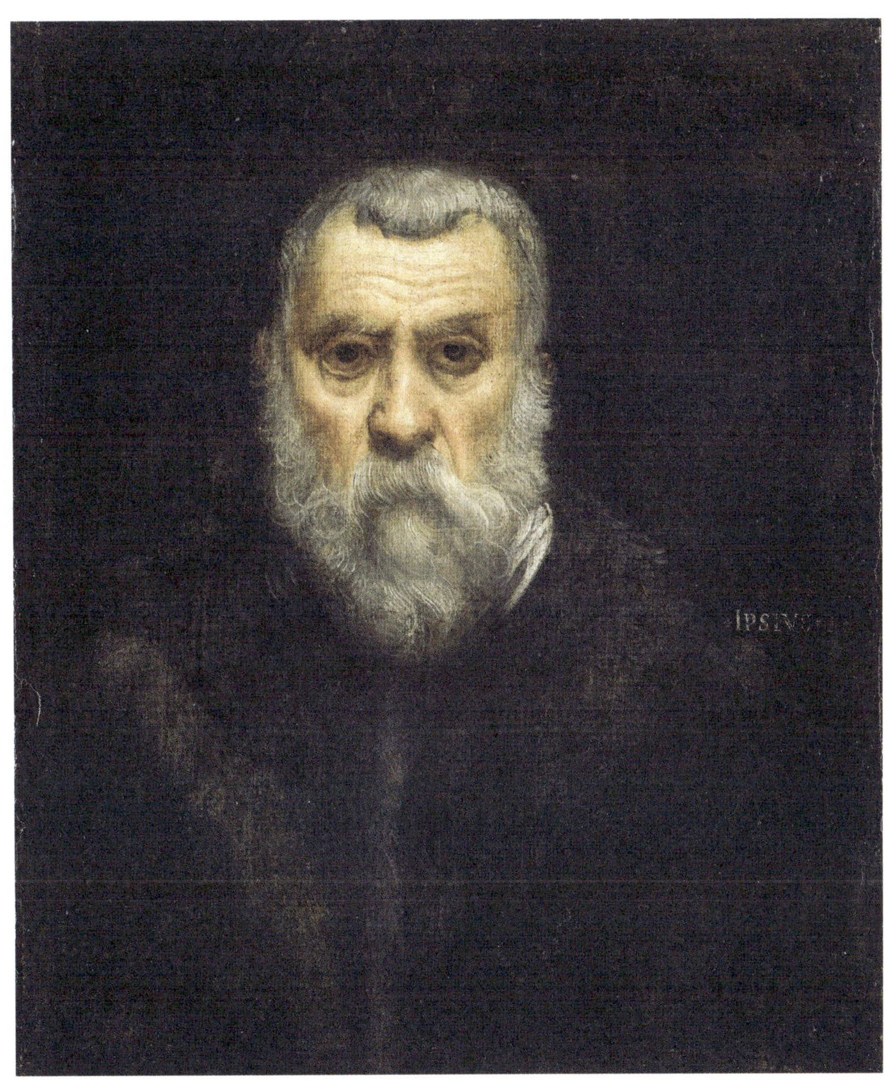

Tintoretto, *Self-portrait*, c. 1588
Louvre, Paris

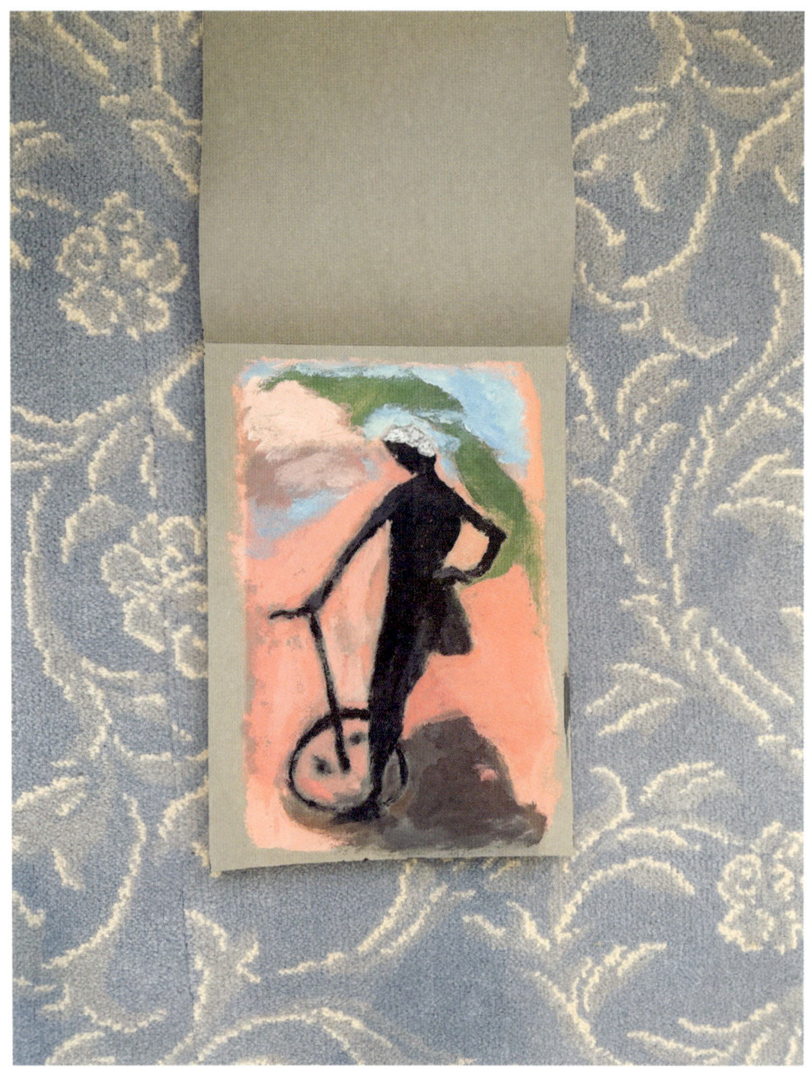

Page from Hodges's sketchbook

many canvases as I could in advance, so that I wouldn't have to worry about carrying all this additional paint. Once I did that, I had what I needed so that, night after night, I could come back to my hotel room and build from and respond to whatever left an impression, whatever excited me, whatever stayed in my mind's eye. And that became a habit. It was like my version of a travel diary, except I was setting up my little rig and painting, and getting lectured by housekeeping to stop getting black all over the furniture and the floors. I didn't have any specific intention other than wanting to respond to what I was seeing.

DG: I was really struck by the immediacy of these paintings. They are records of an instant, a moment, a strong impression.

RBH: Each day—each work—was really built around a reaction to what resonated with me. A lot of this was intuitive, so the work is an emotional reaction. It was me going, *this is the expression, this is the moment, this is what stayed with me*—with no judgment of the end result.

DG: You also had sketchbooks with you. Most artists in the old master tradition would sketch in pen and ink, charcoal, or some kind of graphite, but your sketchbooks are really special because they already contain color.

RBH: I pretty much always have some sort of sketchbook with me, or some way to take account. In this case, because of travel, I kept the size manageable—sketchbooks, index cards, things I could keep in my pocket. Making those very direct drawings and sketches is really free. I wanted to take account of the light, the sensibility of things, because what I was after—what I'm always after—is how it felt. The use of color gives you so much more range to express feeling. I do a lot of work using just graphite or charcoal or oil pastel, but having access to color allowed me to have a broader recollection. And sometimes color was the thing that left the strongest impression.

DG: Where does the exhibition title *Authorities of Reason* come from?

RBH: Titles for me are based on an intuitive feeling. There might be clues and a little archeology in there. *Authorities of Reason* came from the real purpose of this trip: I was seeking something. The entire journey was about seeking, specifically related to the presence, the power, the position that the old masters hold within the canon of image-making. I knew that I was after something and these were the authorities. I was seeking, from those masters, what I could derive from their methods—their exploration provides such a pathway for arriving at a place of mastery.

DG: I like what you are saying about seeking. It's about learning, but it's also a very active and vital relationship. It shows that the old masters' work can still talk to us today. That's in some way how our relationship began—looking at paintings by old masters at the Getty and trying to understand what they might mean for an artist working today, like you.

I'd like to focus on a couple of works from *Authorities of Reason*. One is the almost-monochrome painting *Gaps In The Porcelain (Turin)* (2023), which has a timeless quality—it could even be a marble relief. I see a reclining feminine figure playing a record, which is one of the recurring themes in your works, and she's lying down in a landscape. Looking at this painting, I immediately see it within a specific tradition, a line that goes from Titian to Poussin, Velàzquez, and finally Manet. What was the starting point for this composition?

RBH: I was grappling with the composition of these figures by the old masters. Looking at these works in person, I marveled at how the figures were so monumental—thinking about perspective, how the subjects sit on the horizon line. Regardless of the work's scale, the figures always seem to have this towering power. *Gaps In The Porcelain* is a very formal and traditional depiction of a figure in a landscape. In response to these older works, I was exploring how the space a figure occupies within the picture affects the painting. I was trying to reanimate the elements that I saw as important to the success of those paintings. Going back to titles, with this work I was thinking about porcelain as this incredibly strong—but also very fragile—material, as well as all of its uses throughout history. This includes its relationship to old master works and sculpture. This trip was also the most comprehensive exposure to porcelain in any way that I had ever experienced up to that point. I will leave everything else up for interpretation.

DG: I'm wondering if porcelain is also related to color, here—if you are thinking about white porcelain, and in this monochromatic painting . . . or am I overinterpreting?

RBH: I'm not going to say that you're overinterpreting. But a lot of formal decisions are made in reaction to constraints, so I don't want to make it seem like everything is predetermined. Sometimes a decision will present itself as it's happening and I can recognize, *this is what this means, this is what this is*. I don't want to suggest that a work is fully formed in my head from the moment I put a brushstroke down, because that wouldn't be accurate.

DG: What kind of constraints were you thinking about?

RBH: Such as, how far can I develop this work before I have to roll it up and put it in my suitcase? Imagine running out of materials, what do you have to work with? How much time do you have? What's essential here? What is it that you feel and that you're trying to translate? Those were all really important factors. But these constraints also created a catalyst for freedom, for making in the moment.

DG: Looking at this body of work, I was struck by the fact that in many ways each painting relates to a genre that was typical of the old masters: landscapes, portraits, and still lifes. So what is the balance between recording an impression of reality—a landscape, a view from your hotel room, a café that you frequented—and, in the back of your mind, works by old masters that you are studying in museums?

RBH: I wasn't so concerned about accurately representing a specific thing—my priority was being present in the moment, and casting an image of a sense of the thing.

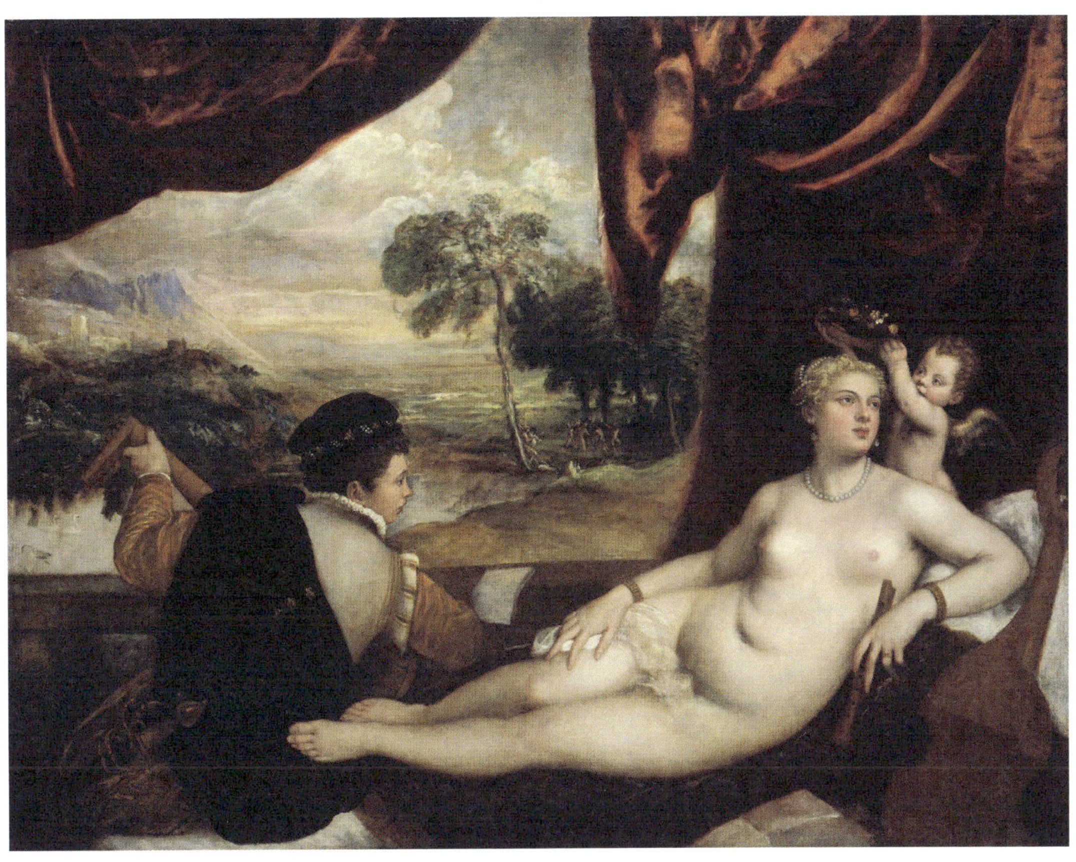

Titian, *Venus and the Lute Player*, c. 1565–70
Metropolitan Museum of Art, New York

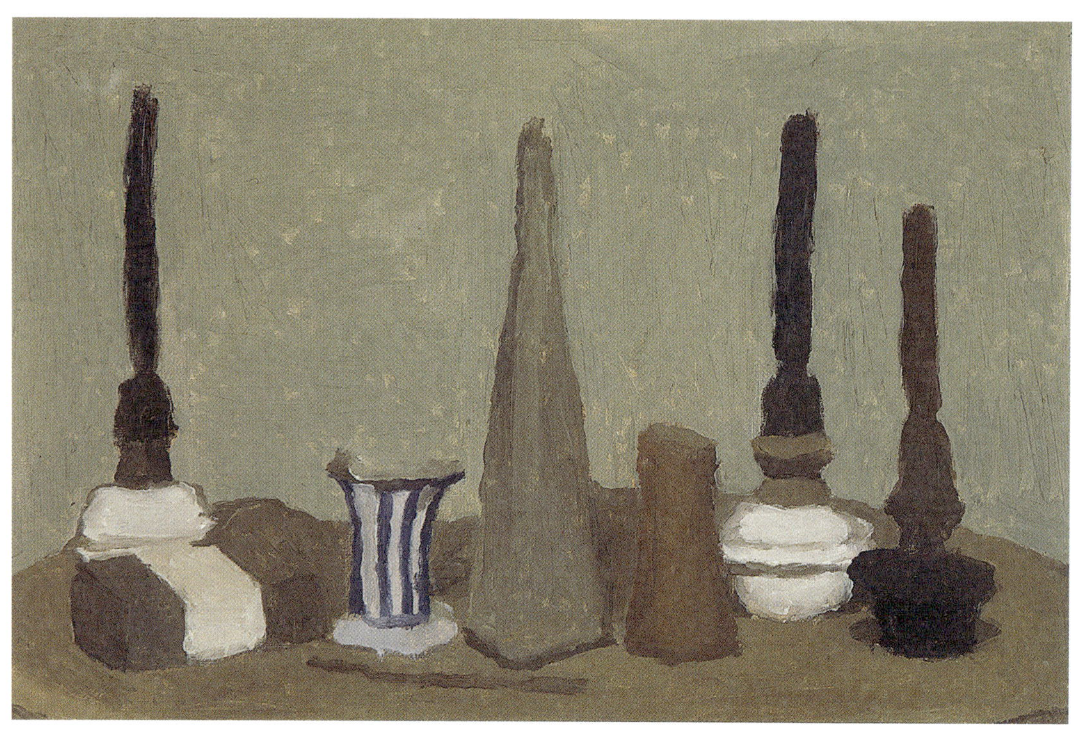

Giorgio Morandi, *Natura morta*, c. 1937–38
Alberto Della Ragione Collection, Museo Novecento, Florence

So I danced between making more representational works and completely abandoning representation. A figure might be based on an impression from reality—meaning someone maybe at a café, or even the presence of a body of work that I saw, where the old masters were handling things in a certain way. All of that affected how I approached a painting.

DG: Your very beautiful, gestural brushwork is truly evident in the pictures in this series, which to me speaks a lot to your encounters with works by the old masters. I see you as being very attracted to the painters in the European tradition who used impasto and visible brushstrokes, like Titian, Rembrandt, Delacroix, with an emphasis on materiality as an embodiment of the presence of the hand of the artist.

RBH: I think one of the most fascinating pieces for me was being able to see what I called the humanity of the work—as you're looking deeply into these paintings, you can appreciate the brushstrokes, the hand of the artist. Up close, I could see the making, and envision how I make, and draw some connections to the experience—the quadrillion decisions that are made in terms of the application of paint and the give and take that happens in trying to bring forth and make an image.

DG: You also take very individual photographs. They capture a shape, a color, a motif. What role does photography play for you when you're painting?

RBH: Photography forces me to look at the world in a very specific way, with a certain lens or filter. But there is a distinct difference—when I'm painting, I am definitely going against the grain of the photograph as a tool. Photos capture that event, that moment, that reality, like it exists. When I'm painting, I'm not after what the thing looked like, I'm after the spirit of a moment.

DG: But some of your photographs capture—in something that is real—an abstract quality, a form, a shape, a color, that resonates with the character of your paintings.

RBH: Well, I studied theater and film, so I would imagine that when it comes to photography, I'm looking at my surroundings from the perspective of a cinematographer or director. I can certainly plug into that affinity, that part of my development. If I'm going to take a picture, it's usually because there's a certain sensibility—it could be shape, light, shadow—that draws me to try to capture that moment.

DG: We have spoken before about your love for Giorgio Morandi. You visited his house and studio in Bologna. What does Morandi do for you?

RBH: Morandi, for me, is like how in music there are songs that make you go, *Man, I wish I could have written that*. The simplicity and warmth and humanity of what Morandi could do . . . Also, the repetition—

DG: Almost an obsession.

RBH: Yes, obsession. Looking at Morandi's work, I can understand and envy it, and I also have this appreciation for arriving somewhere that only comes through experiencing that journey, where you aren't continuously staying married to an idea and a practice and are instead watching it continue to evolve and be distilled. When I was at his house, looking at the objects with my naked eye, I tried to imagine how Morandi arrived at assembling and representing his subjects, as well as how his compositions became so beautifully refined. I was also thinking how beautiful it must have been to have thought that way. So that was another part of the trip: going to the artists' homes, the places where the work was made. I was seeing objects that I had only seen in books—they are there the way that the artist might have left them.

DG: In the Pinacoteca di Brera in Milan, you stopped in front of these detached mural paintings by Bramante—quintessential Renaissance works. What struck you there?

RBH: I was often stopped in my tracks by how a surface or formal element was approached and how that differed from a misconception or a preconceived notion of how something was done. What drew me to those works was how matte and chalky they appear, which was so different than everything else around them. Even without a gloss, there was so much detail and depth—I was marveling at the fact that this was paint rather than pastel. I loved the softness and the tone of these works, and how he achieved so much vibrancy and detail. I couldn't stop looking, and looking for reasons and answers.

DG: You were also looking at the incredible, almost tactile precision with which Bramante depicts curls . . .

RBH: Yeah, it's like a magic trick.

DG: They look like they are sculpted in metal. You explained the qualities that appealed to you very well, but initially I was surprised that you liked the Bramante frescoes. I feel that you are usually attracted to the seventeenth century, with its strong contrasts of light and shadow—in some way to the dark side of Italian painting—rather than to the luminous geometry of the Renaissance.

RBH: You might be able to identify that in me more than I'm able to. But there is something about the frescoes by Bramante—I have such an appreciation for what it takes to present works of that character. I love taking all of that in and then deconstructing the parts that are pertinent to my own practice and drawing connections.

DG: It was the ideal European grand tour, but also extremely personal. And I enormously enjoyed the exhibition, so thank you very much, Reggie.

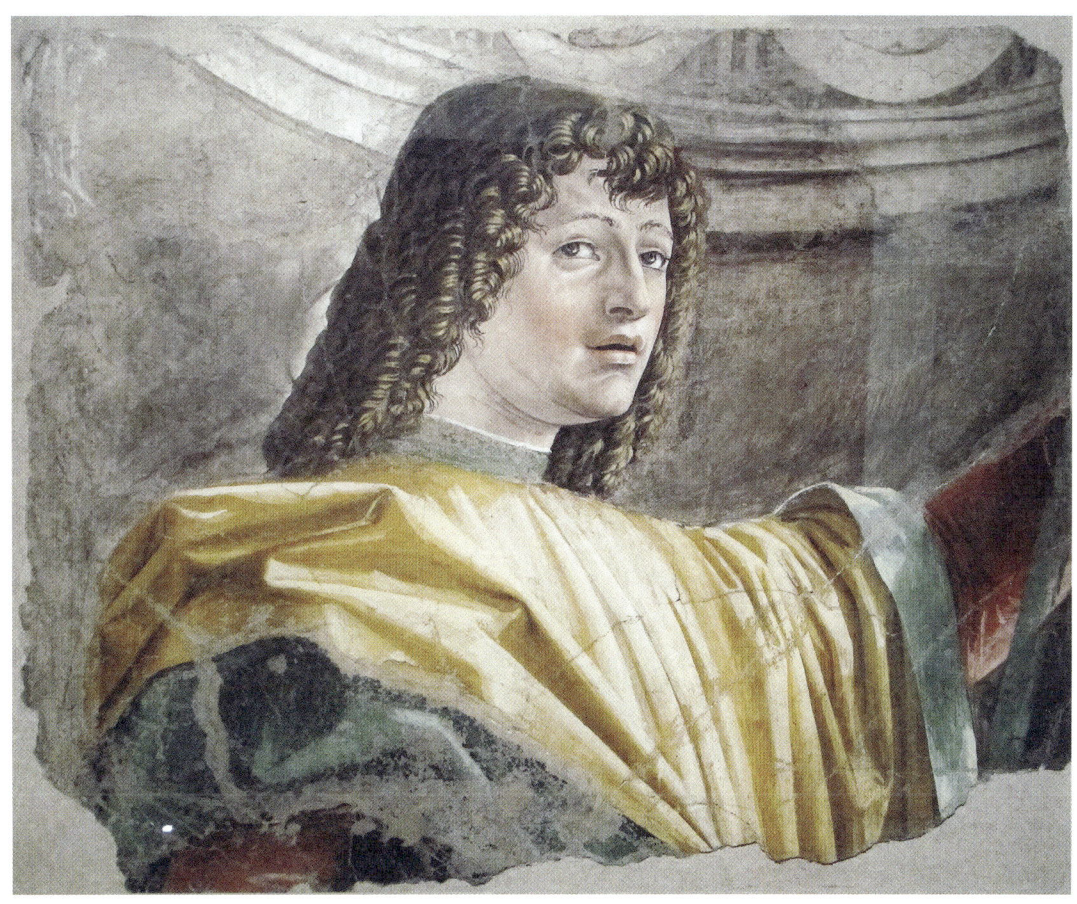

Donato Bramante, *Uomo dall'alabarda* (Man with Halberd), 1486–87
Pinacoteca di Brera, Milan

# Plates

# Amsterdam

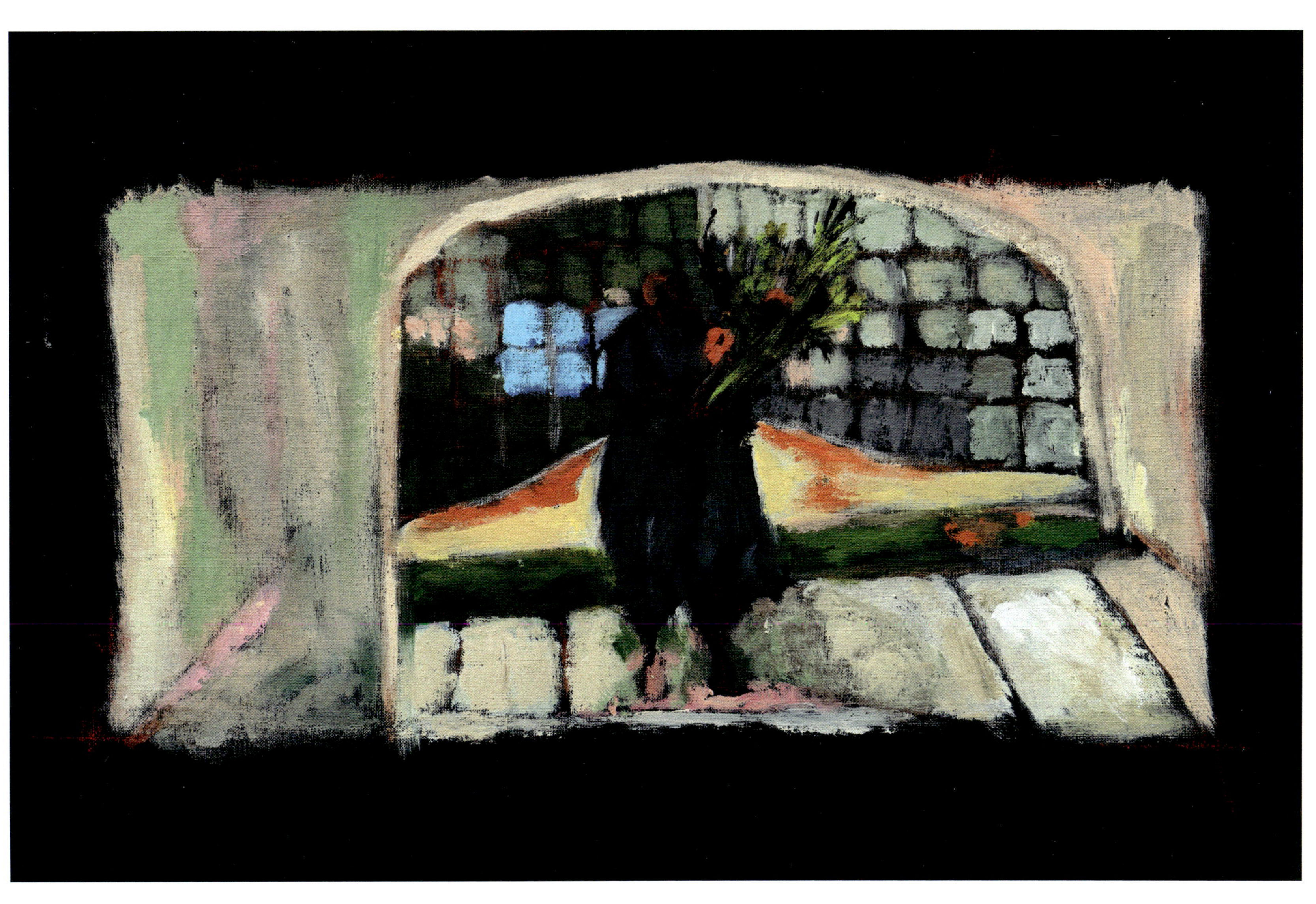



*Stepping Stone (Amsterdam)*, 2023

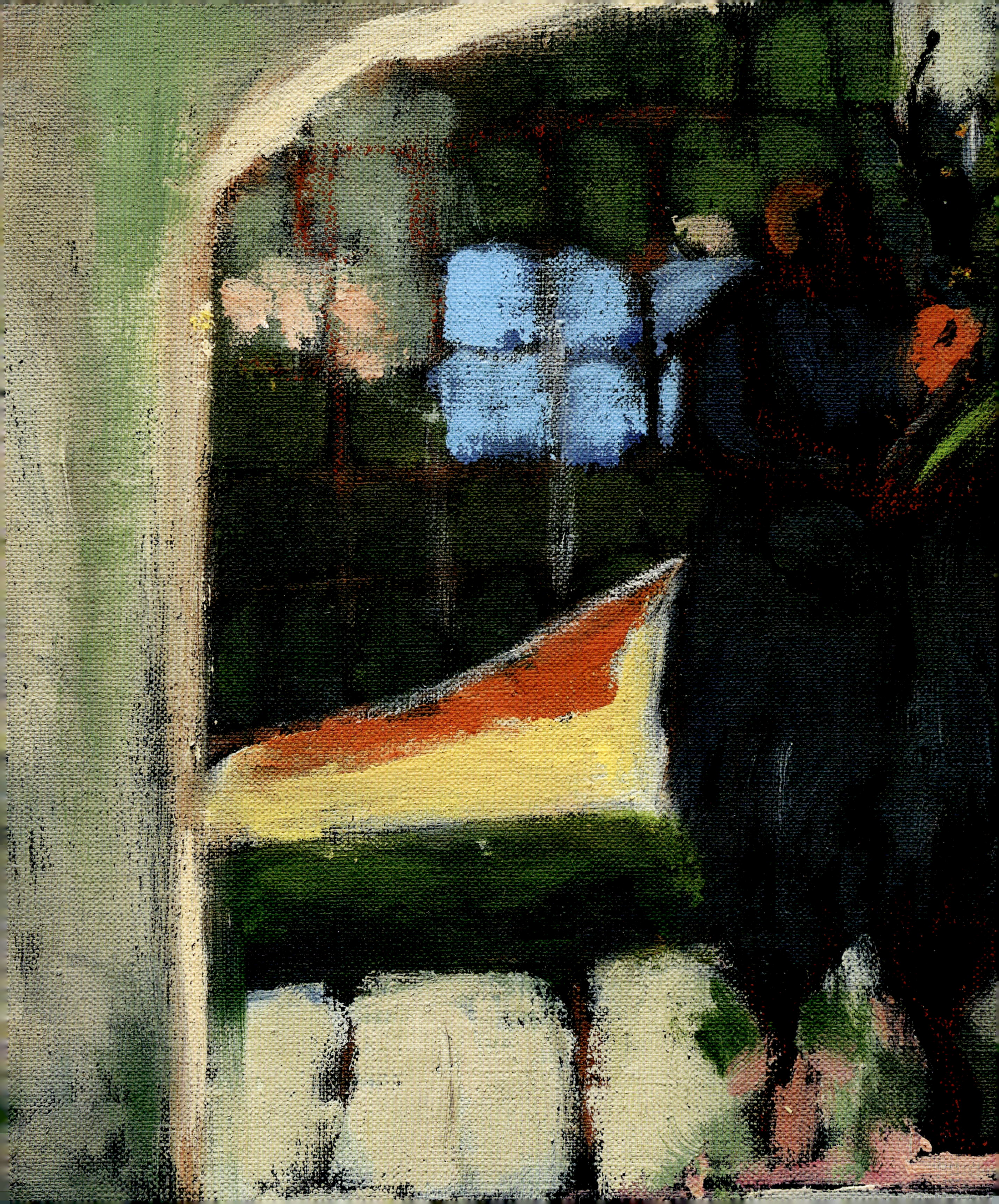

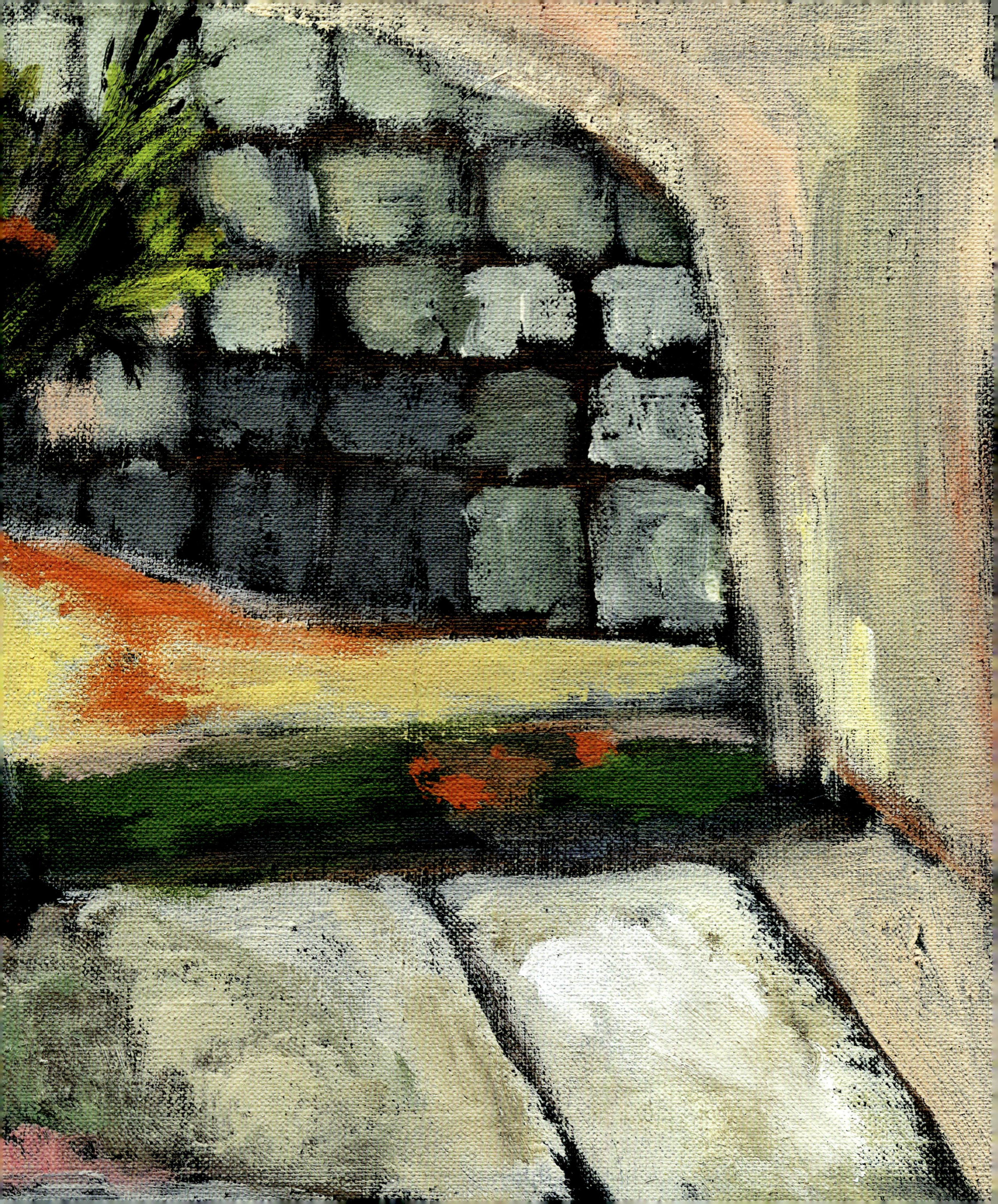

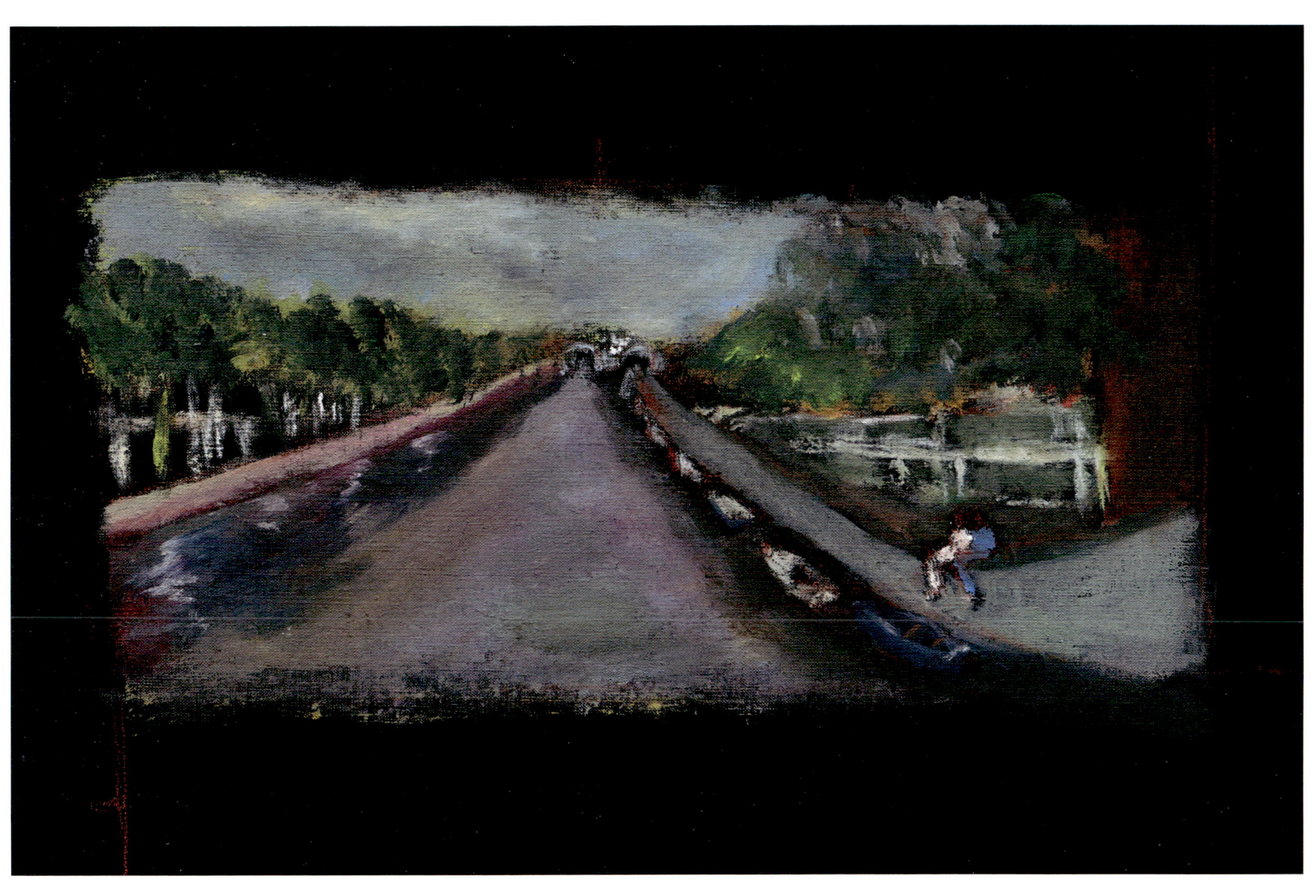



*Thickly Settled (Amsterdam)*, 2023

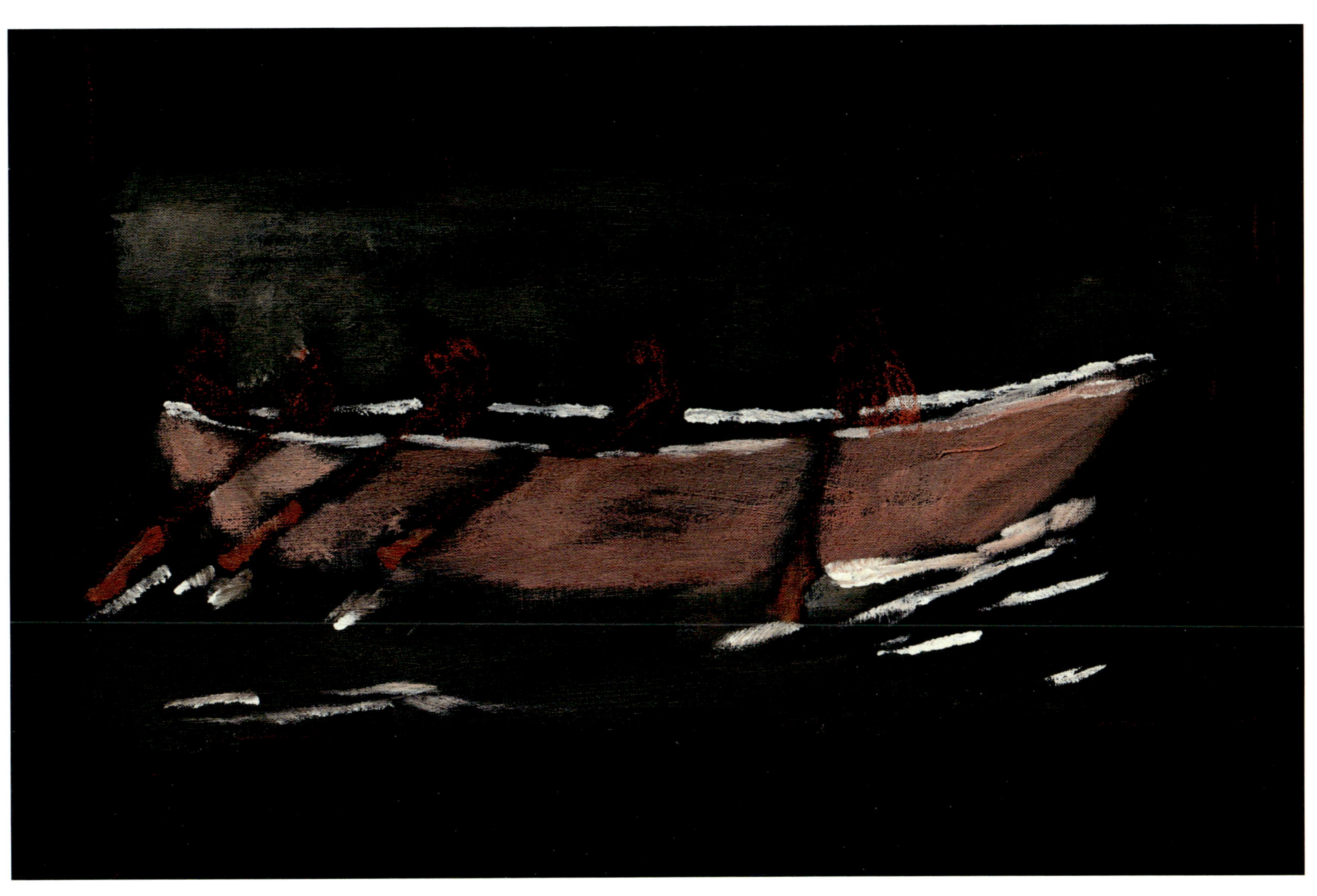



*Low Clearance (Amsterdam)*, 2023

# London

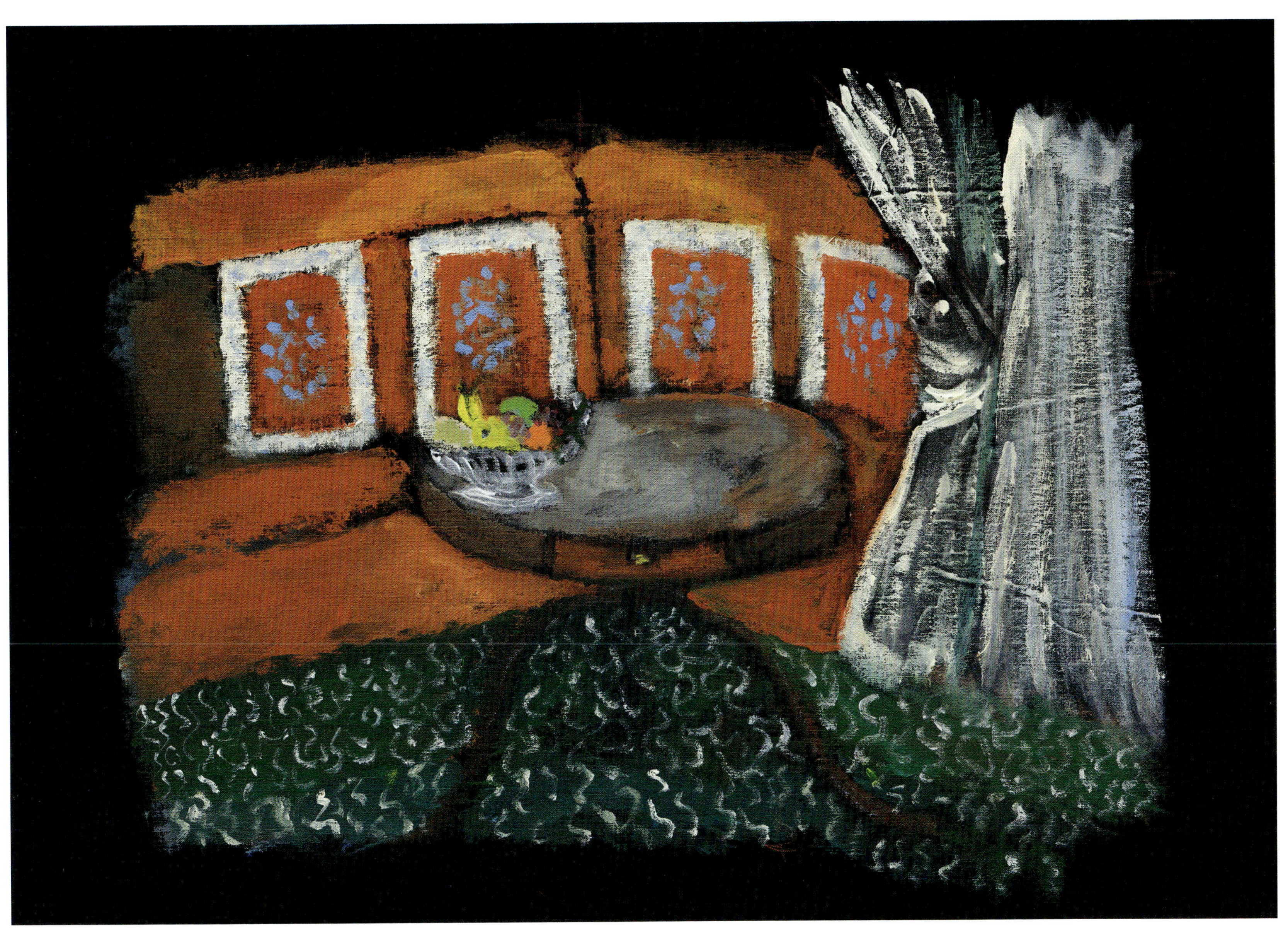

*Truffle Season (London)*, 2023

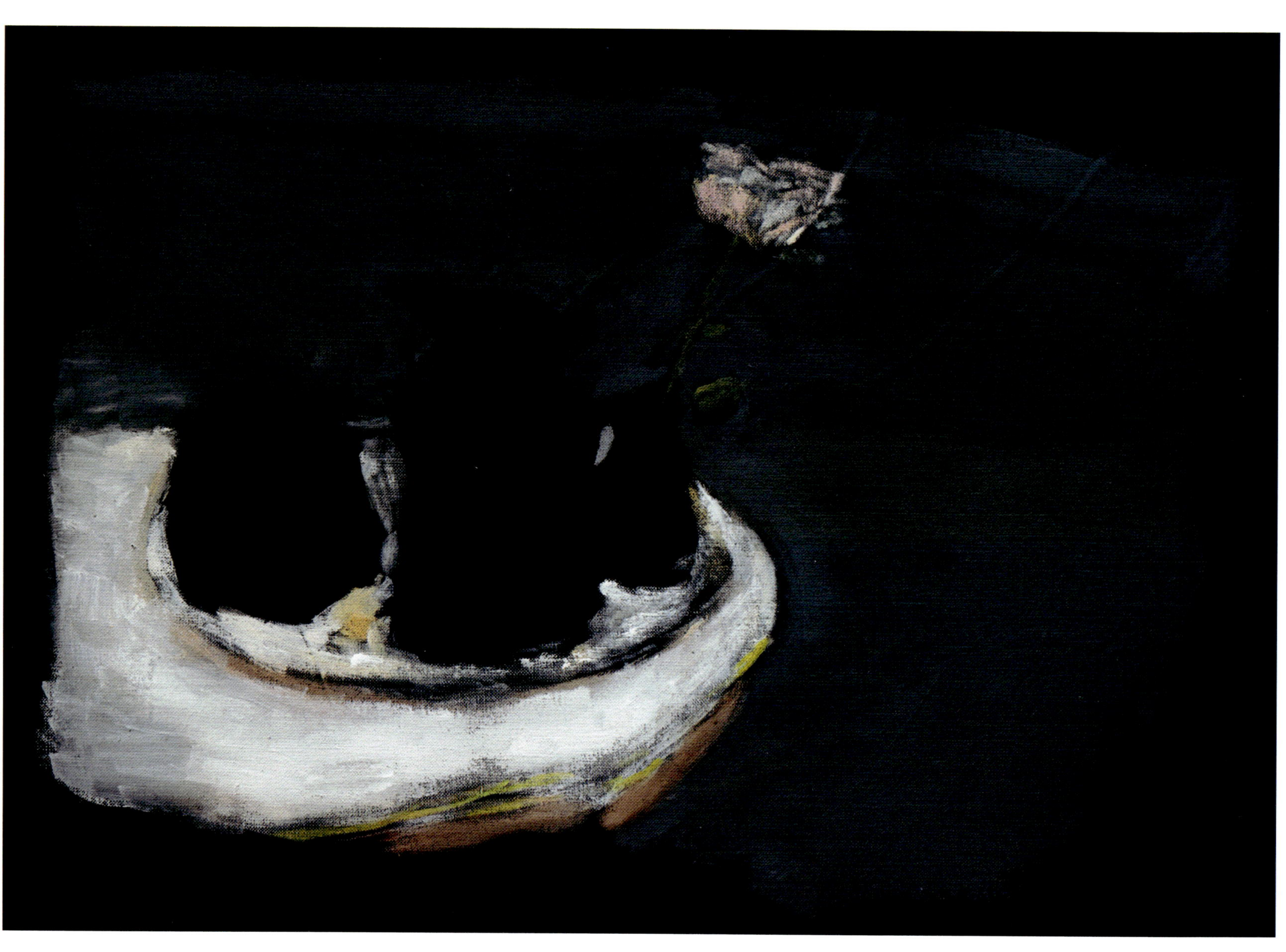

*Dances Out Of Time (London)*, 2023

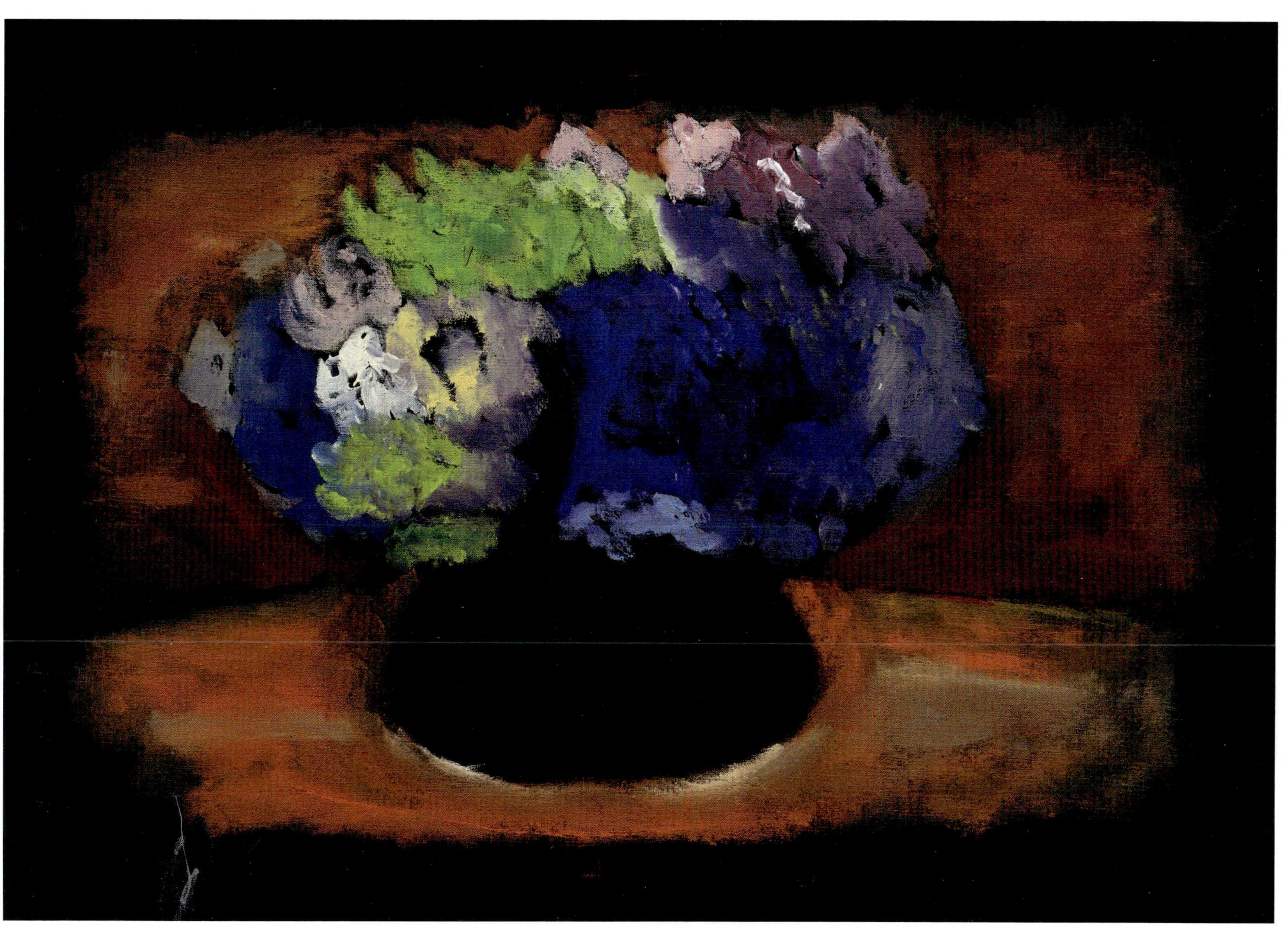



*Level Ground (London)*, 2023

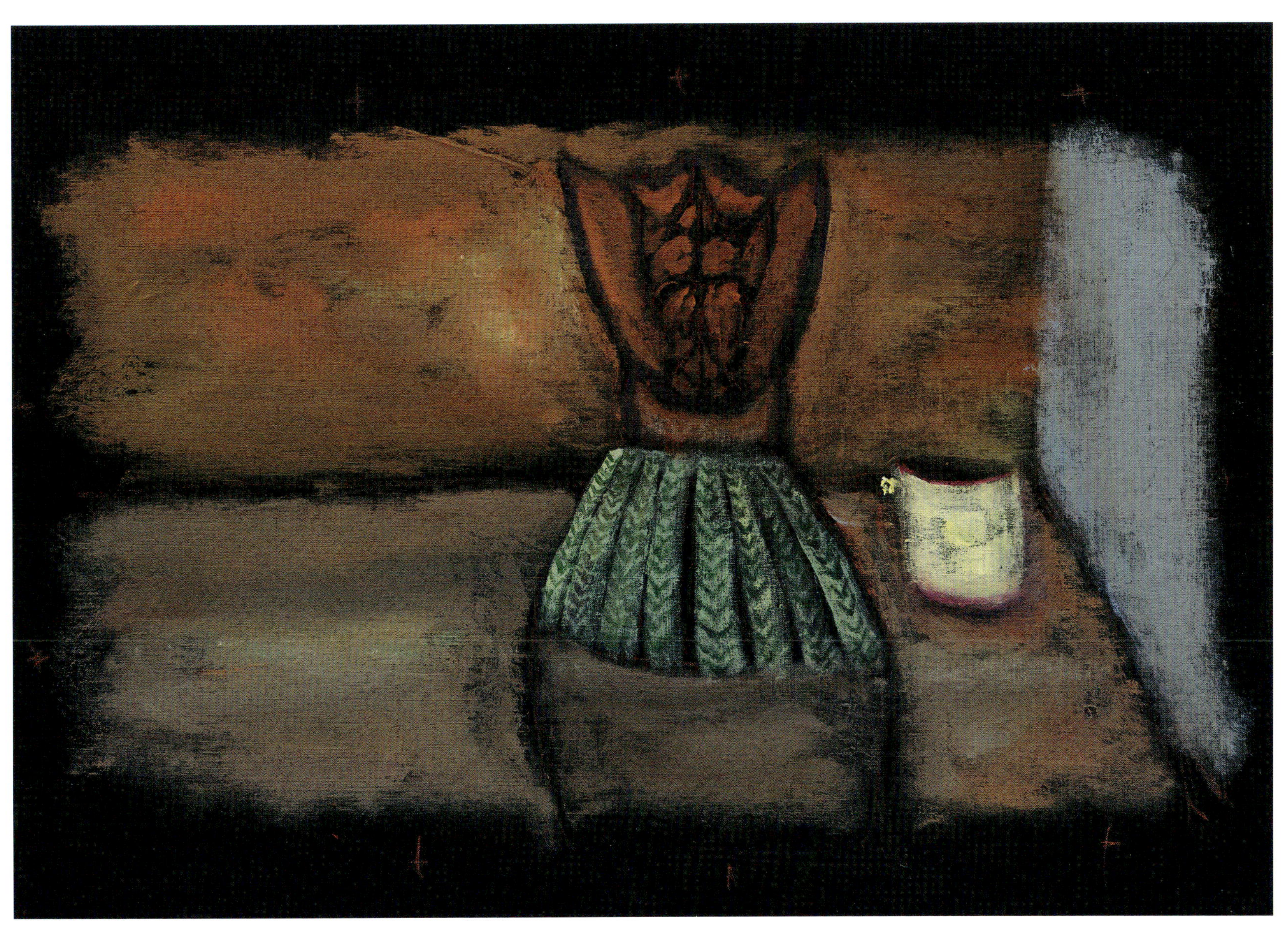



*Coursed Out (London)*, 2023

Paris

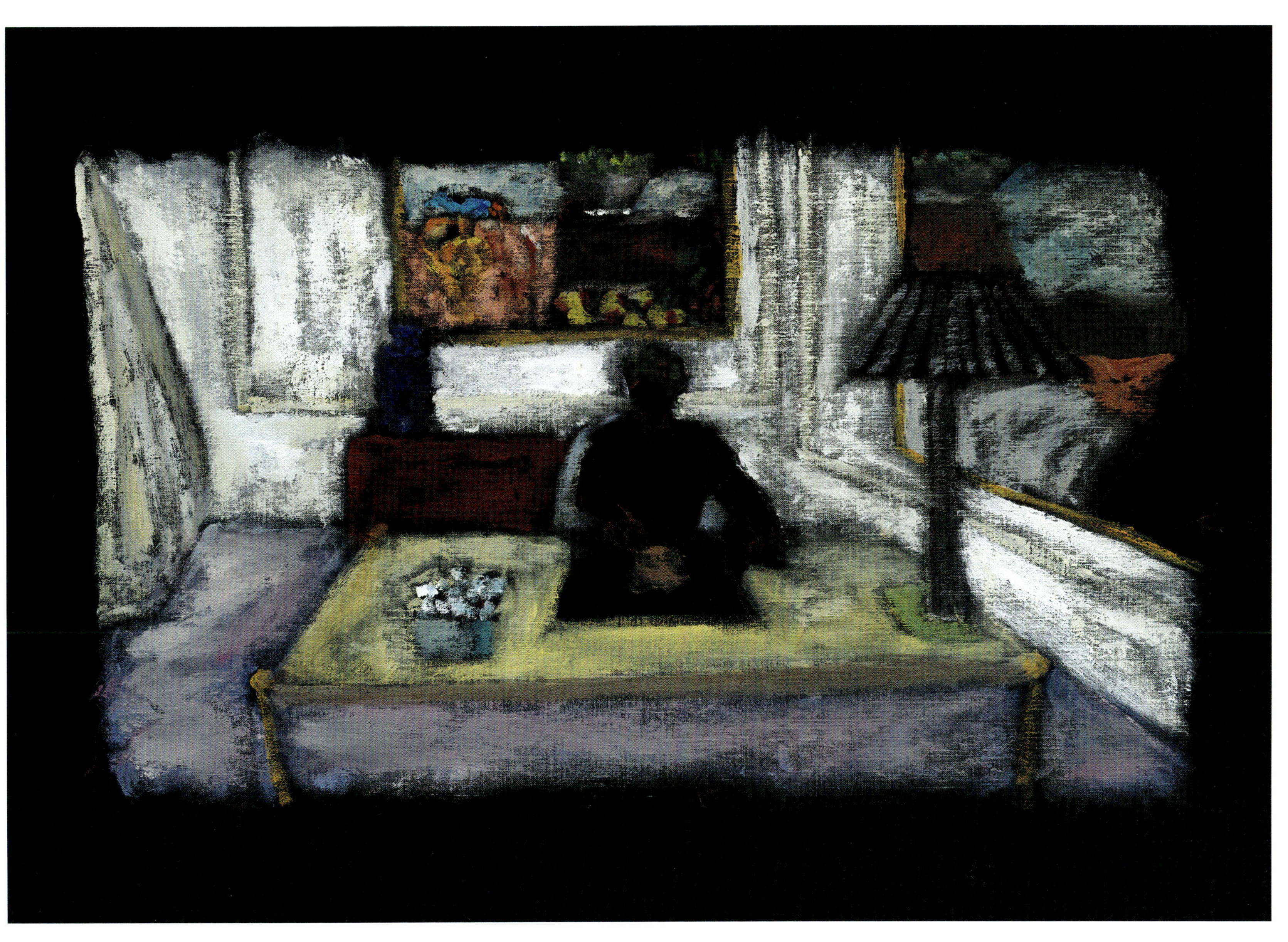



*Golden Triangle (Paris)*, 2023

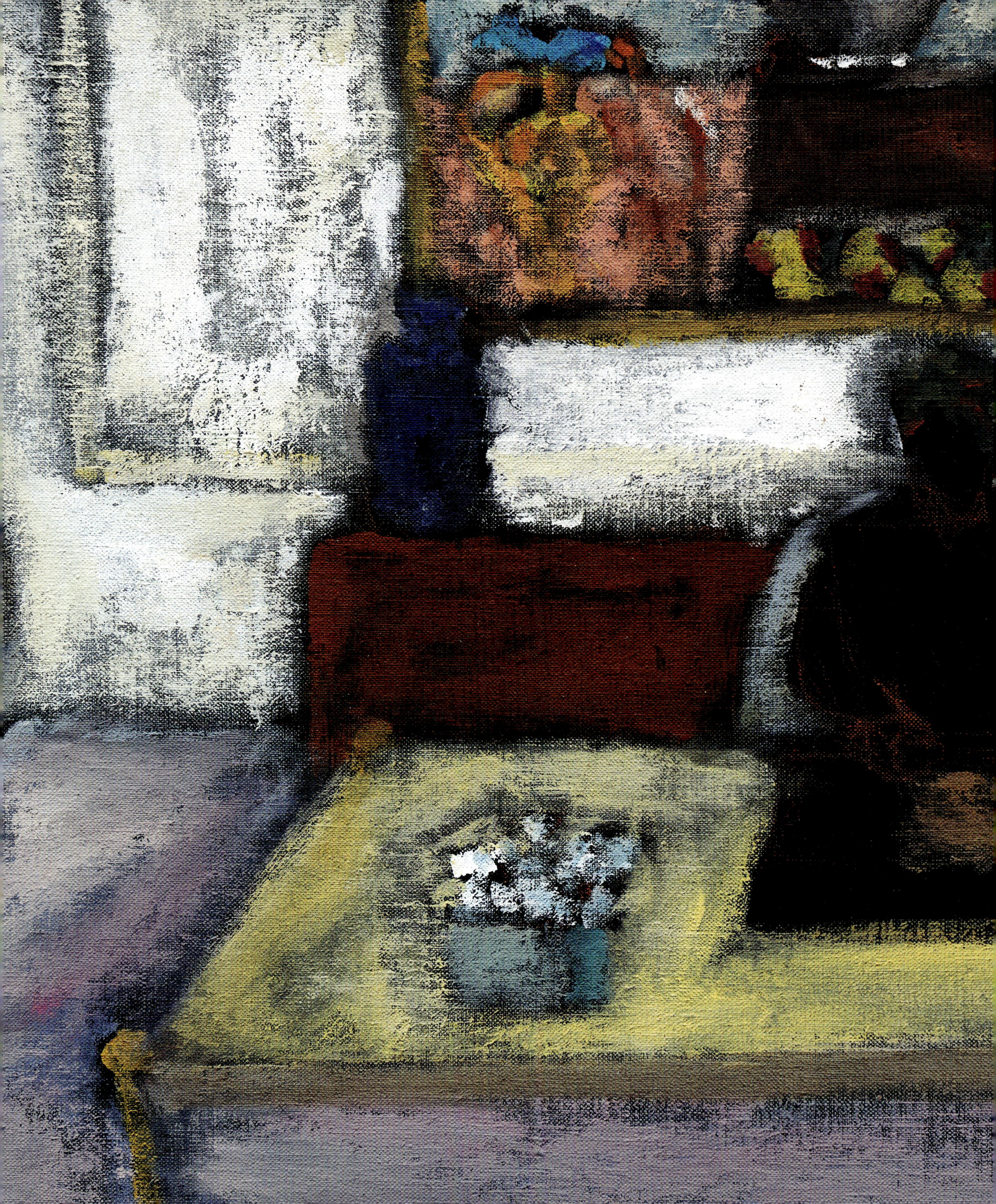

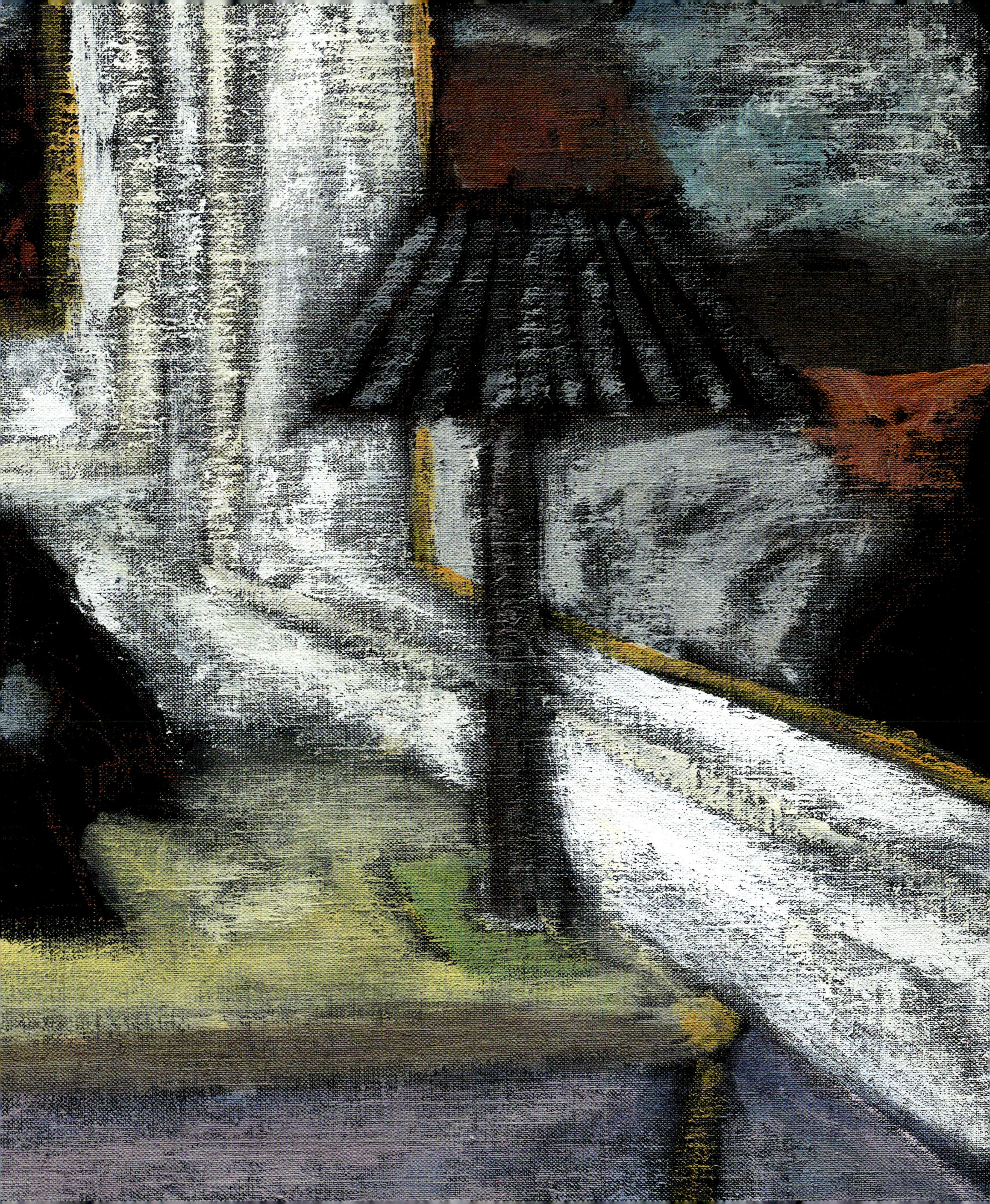

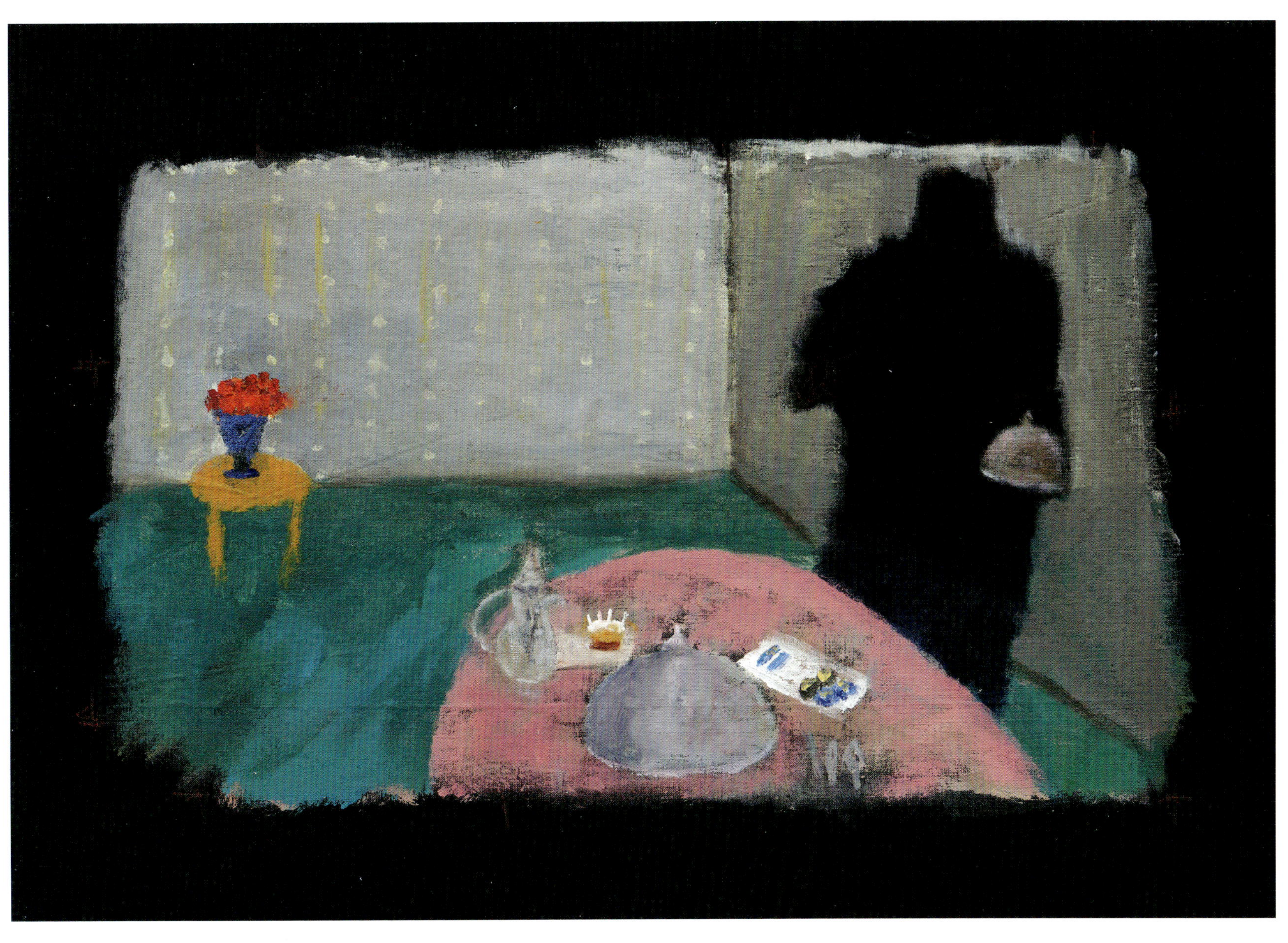



*Triomphe (Paris)*, 2023

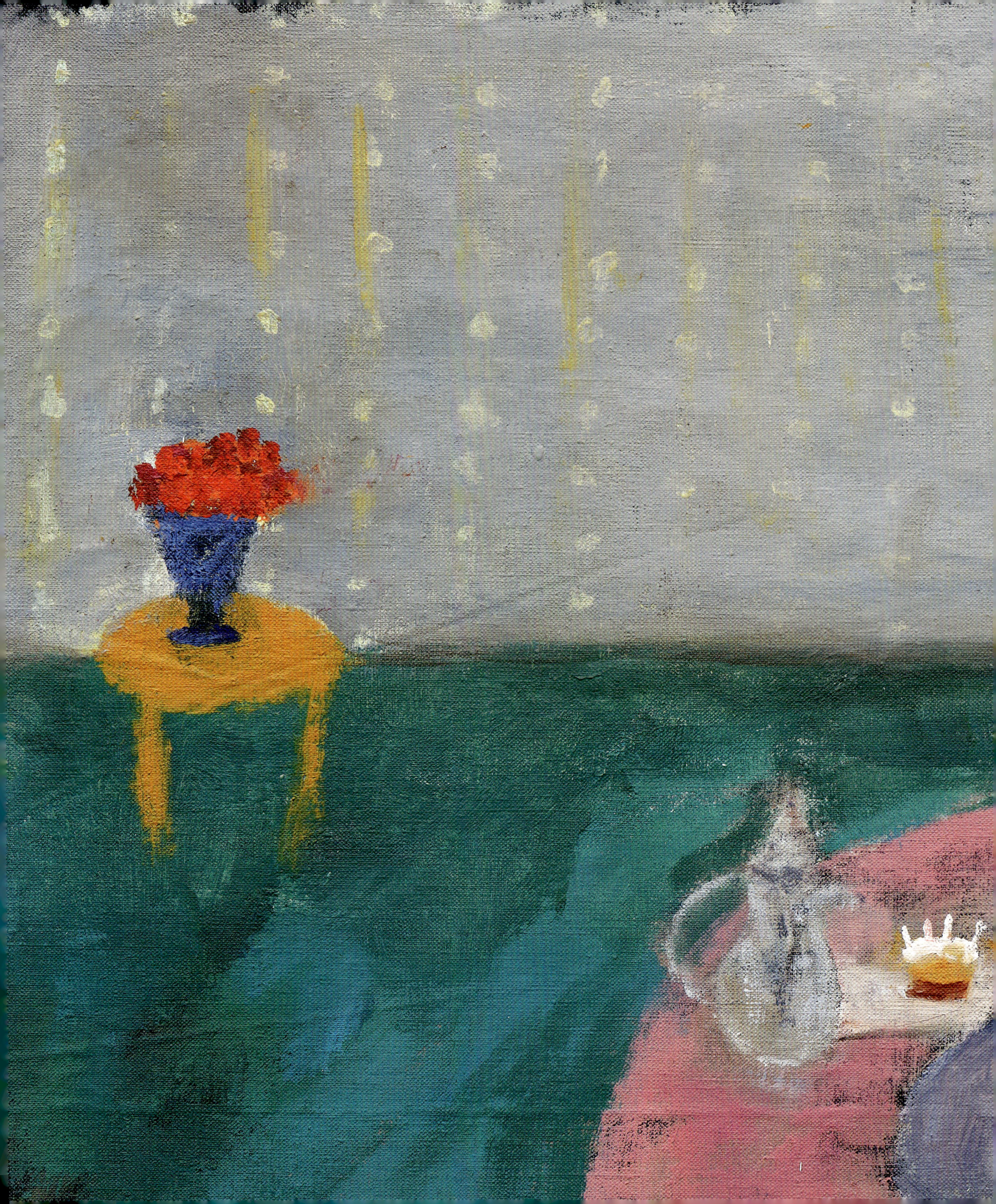

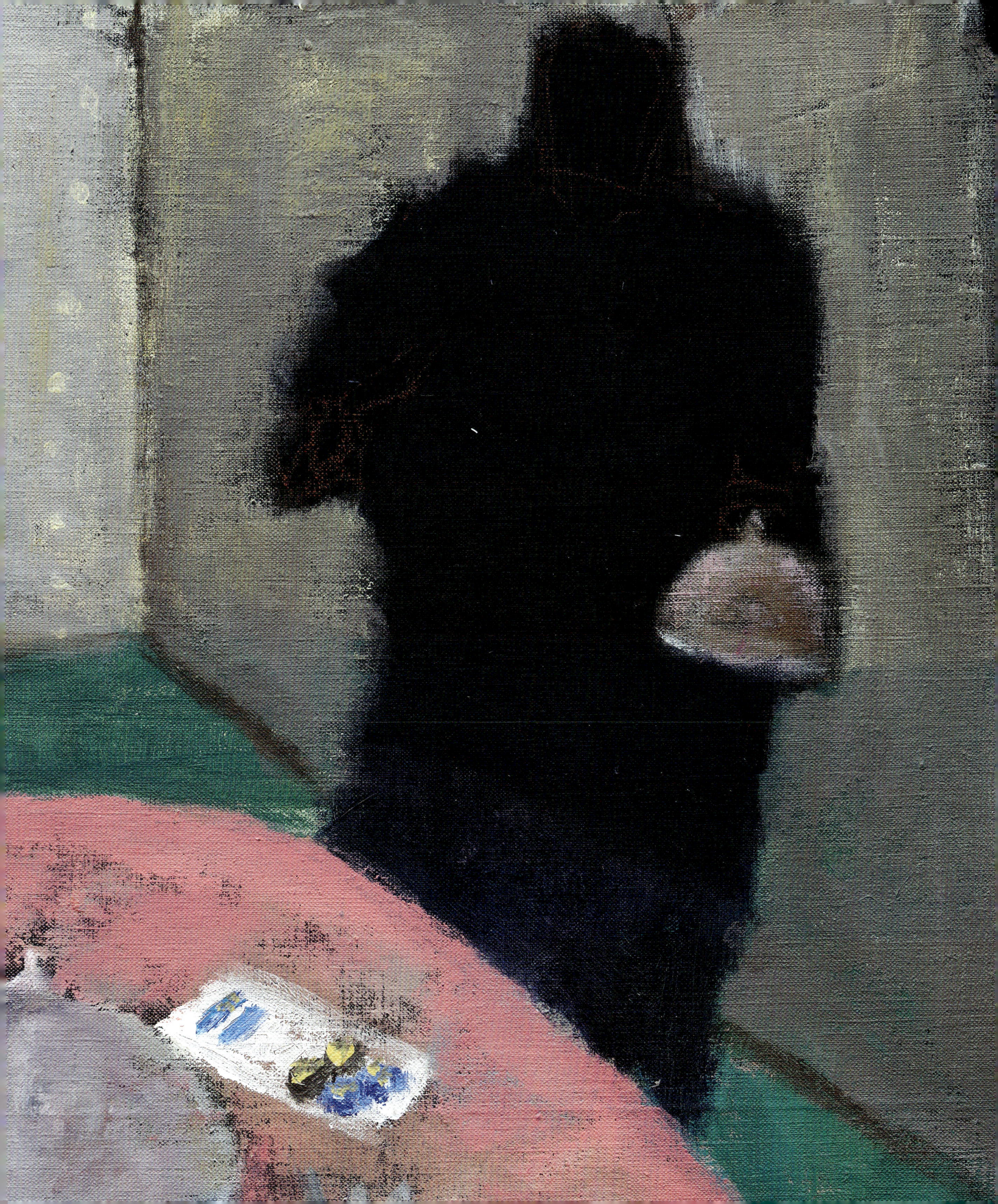

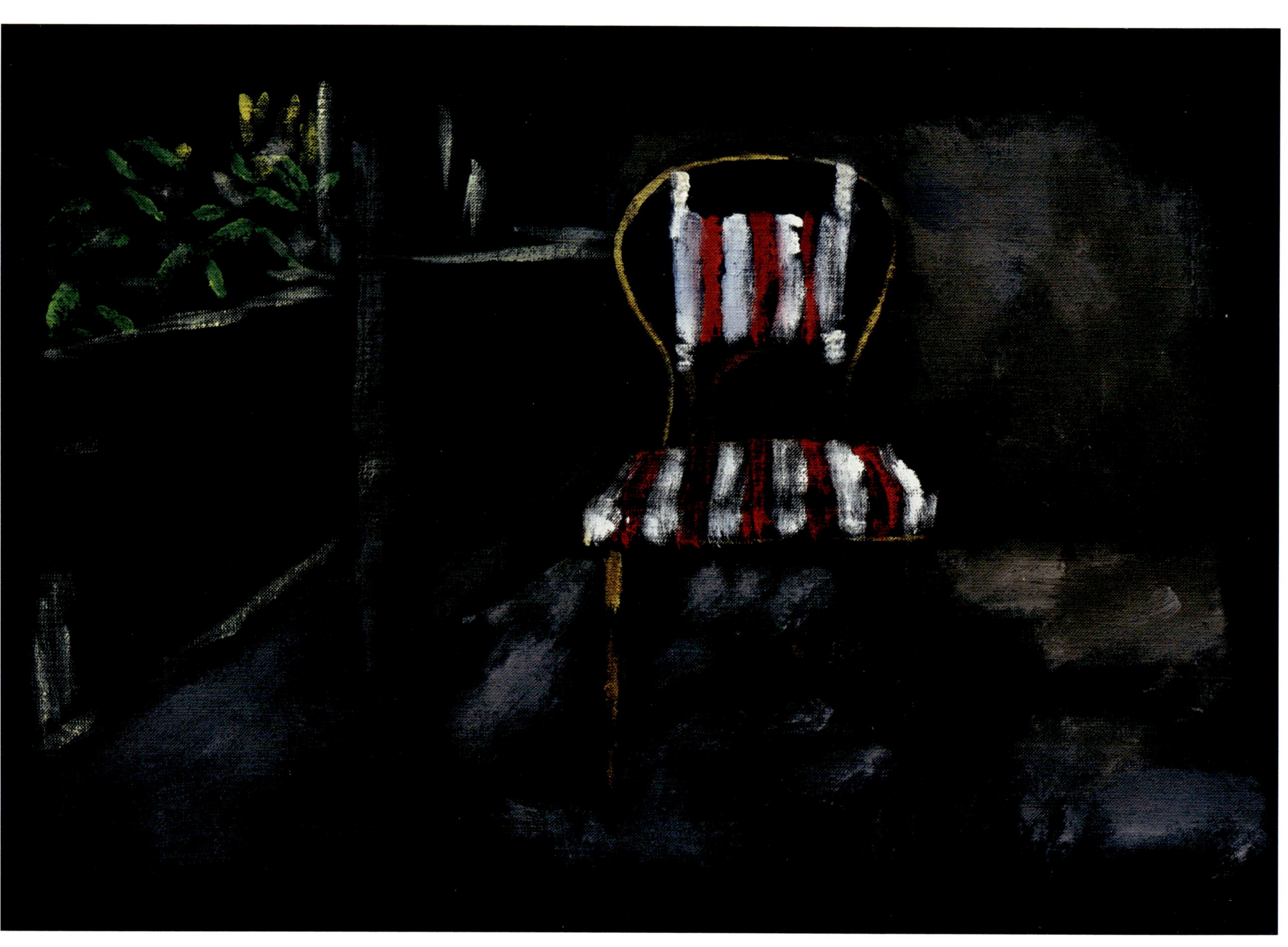

*Single Ticket (Paris)*, 2023

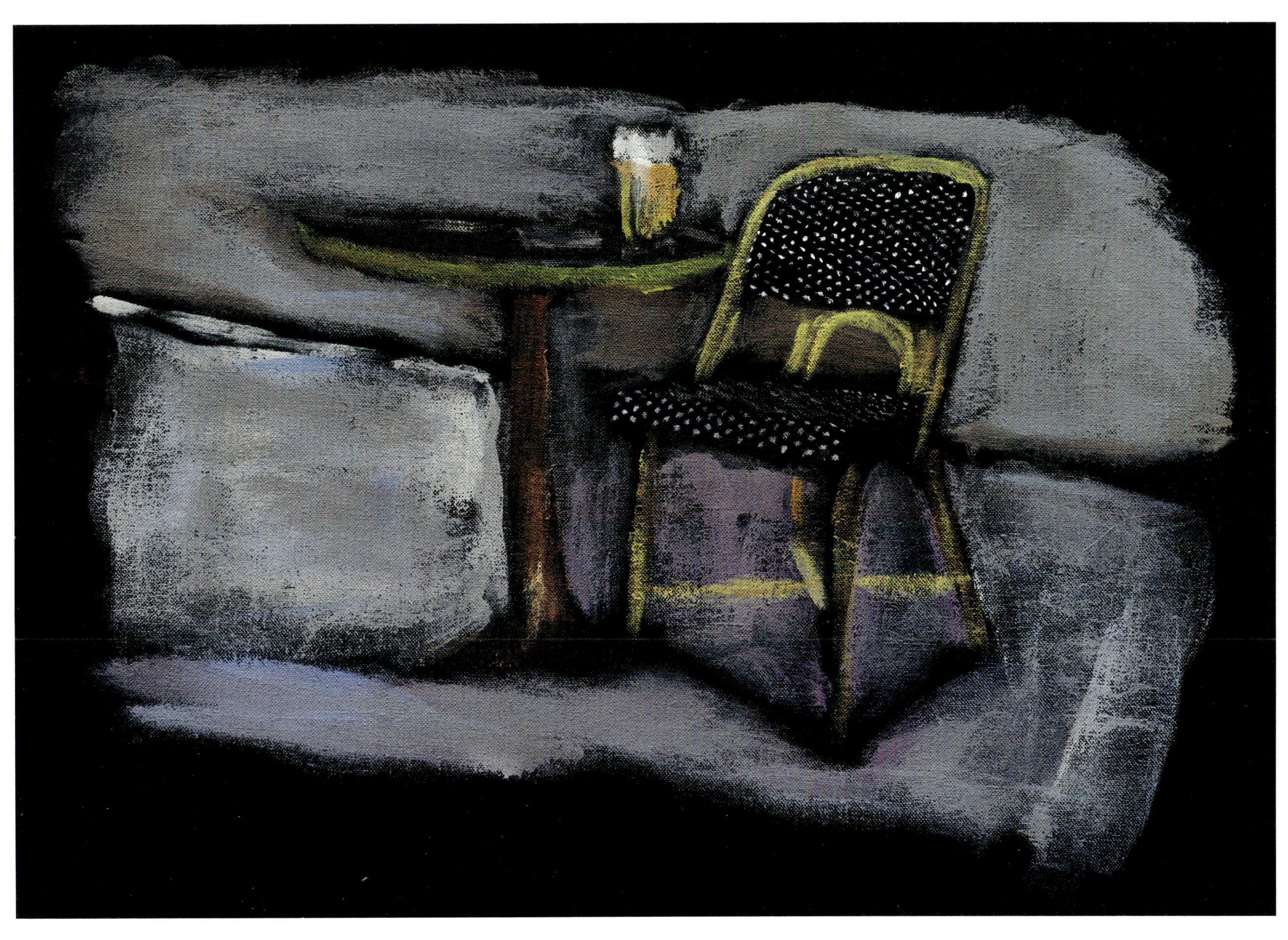



*Signature (Paris)*, 2023

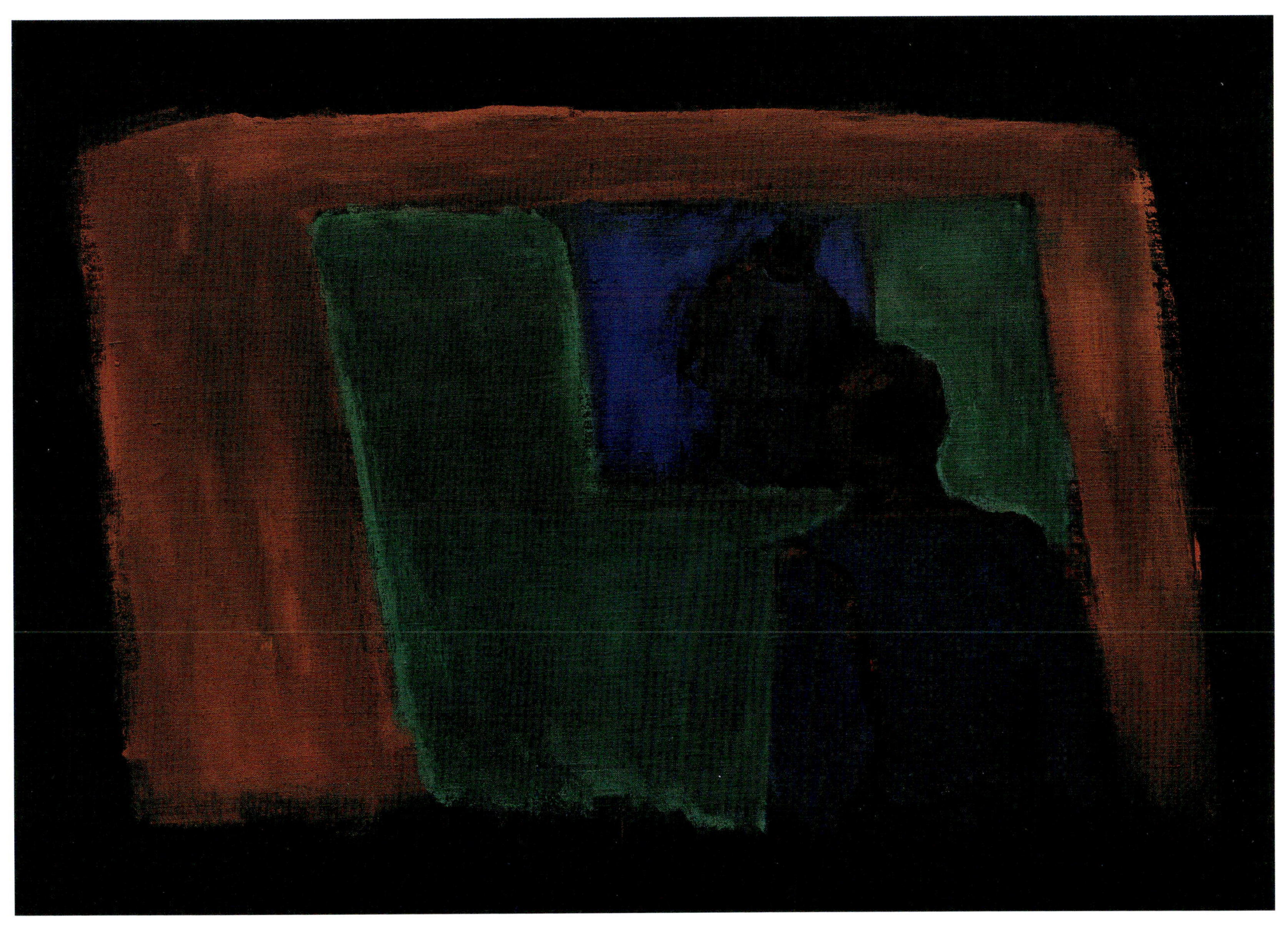



*The Duet (Paris)*, 2023

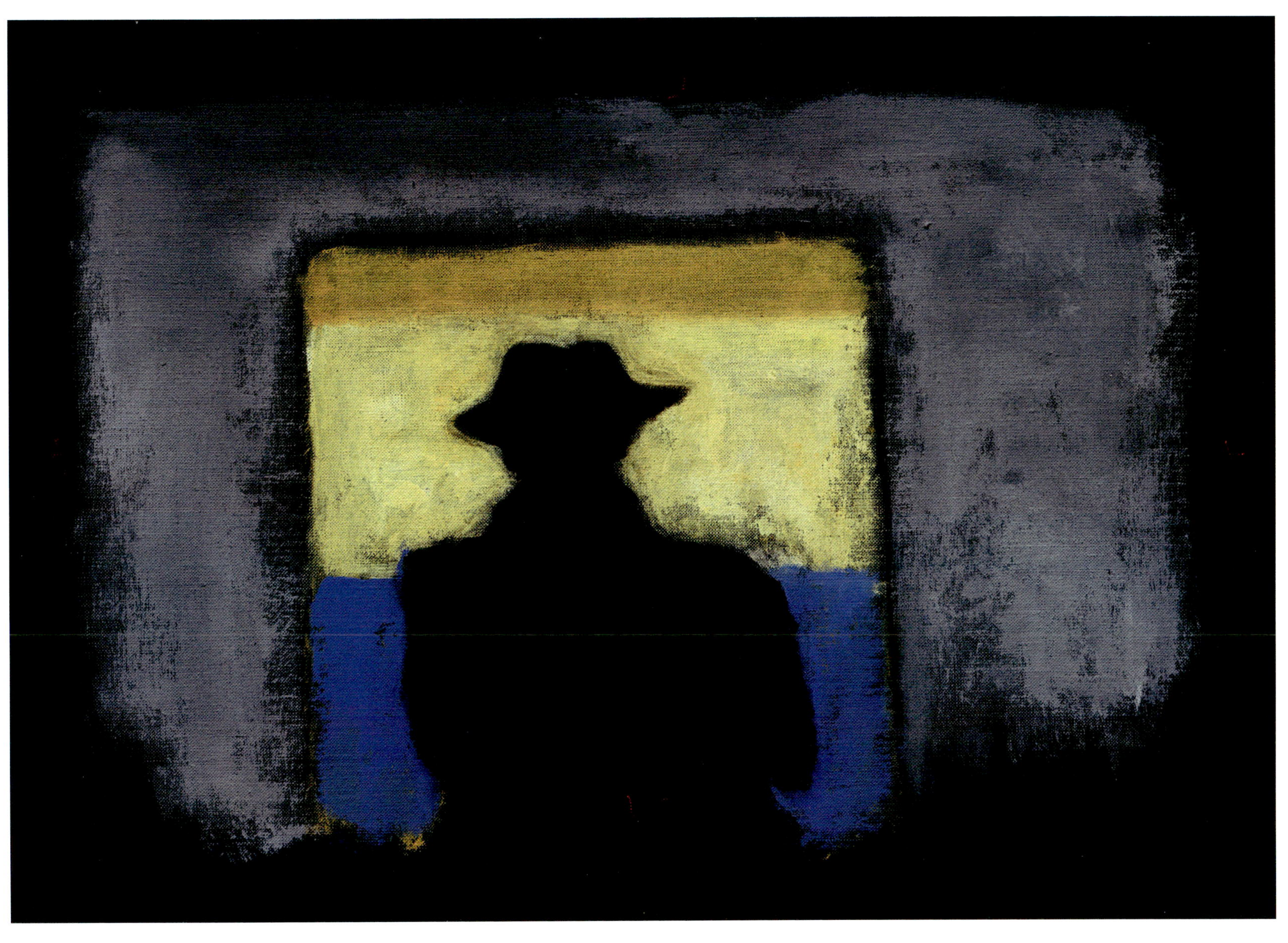

*Wordless (Paris)*, 2023

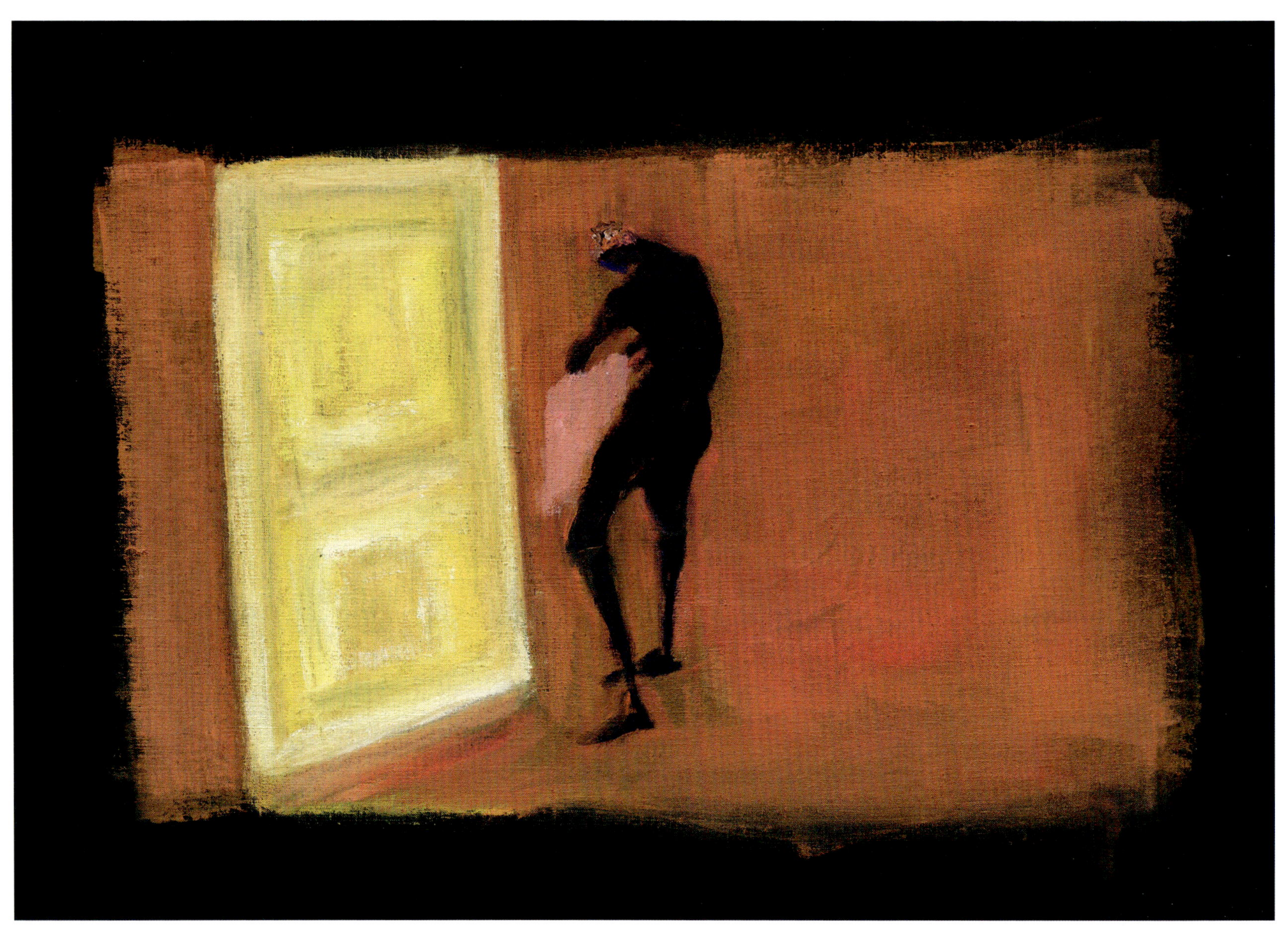



*Rosewood (Paris)*, 2023

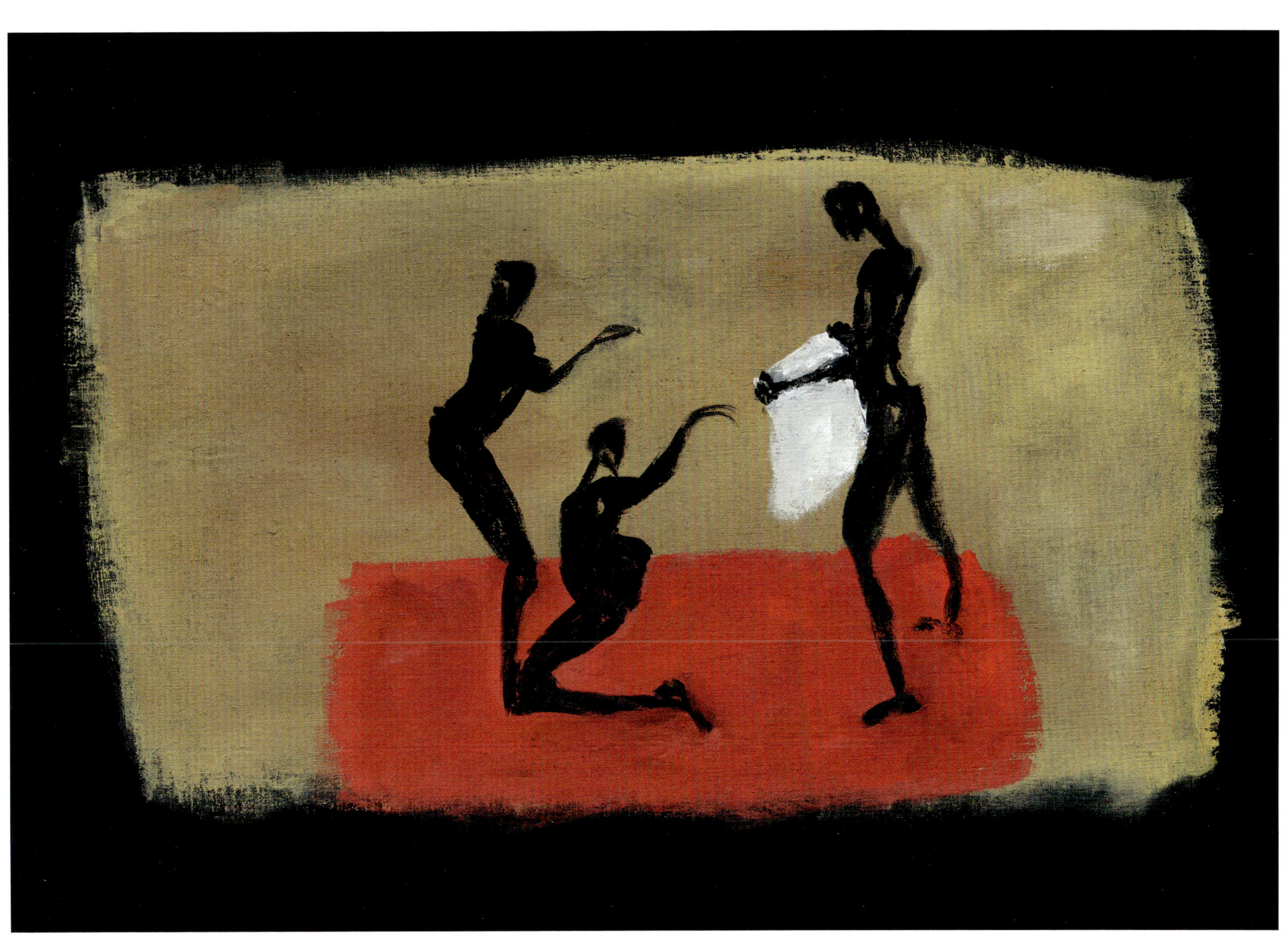

     *Calm Crillon (Paris)*, 2023

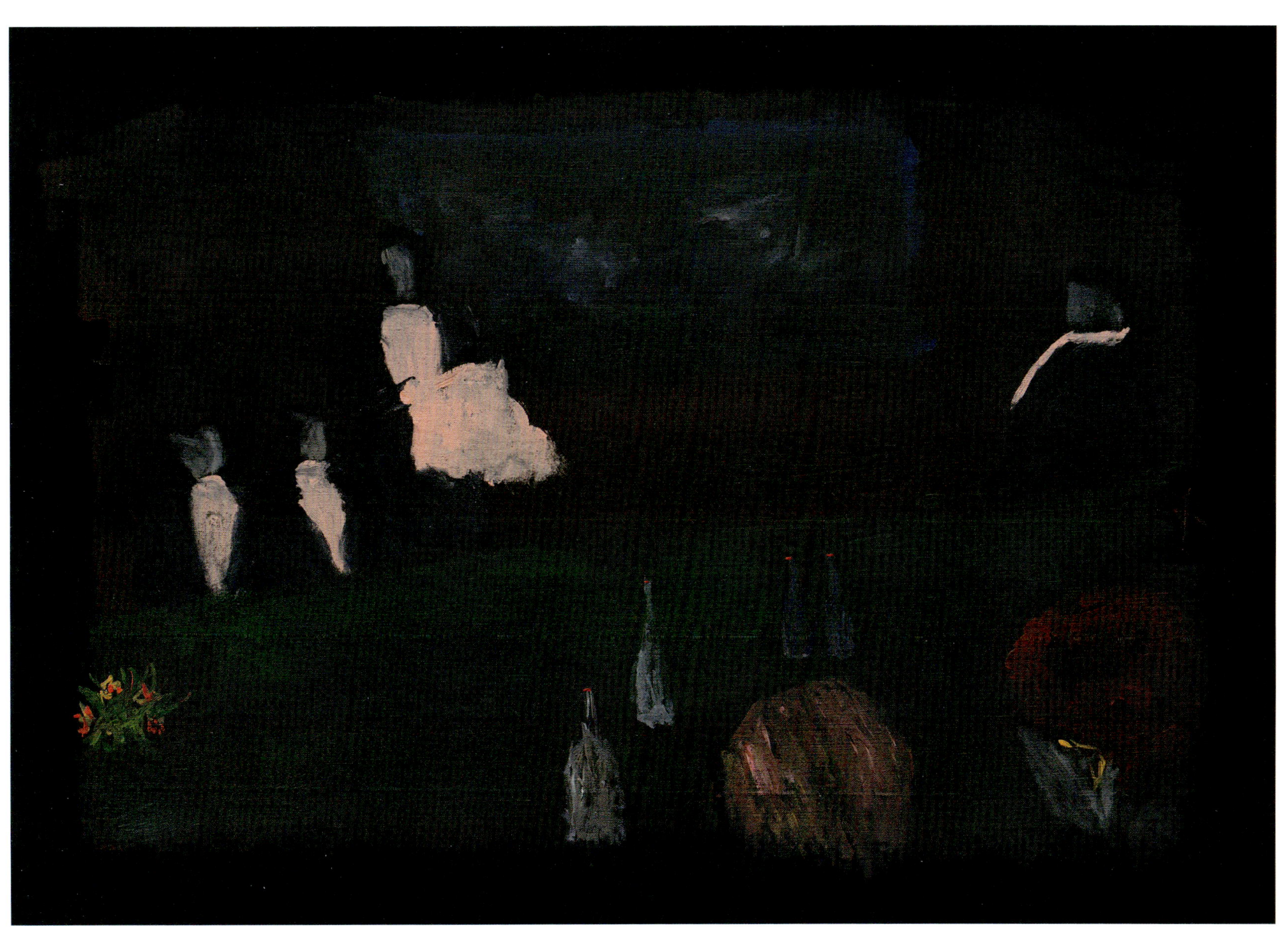



*Impetus For The Gala (Paris)*, 2023

# Berlin

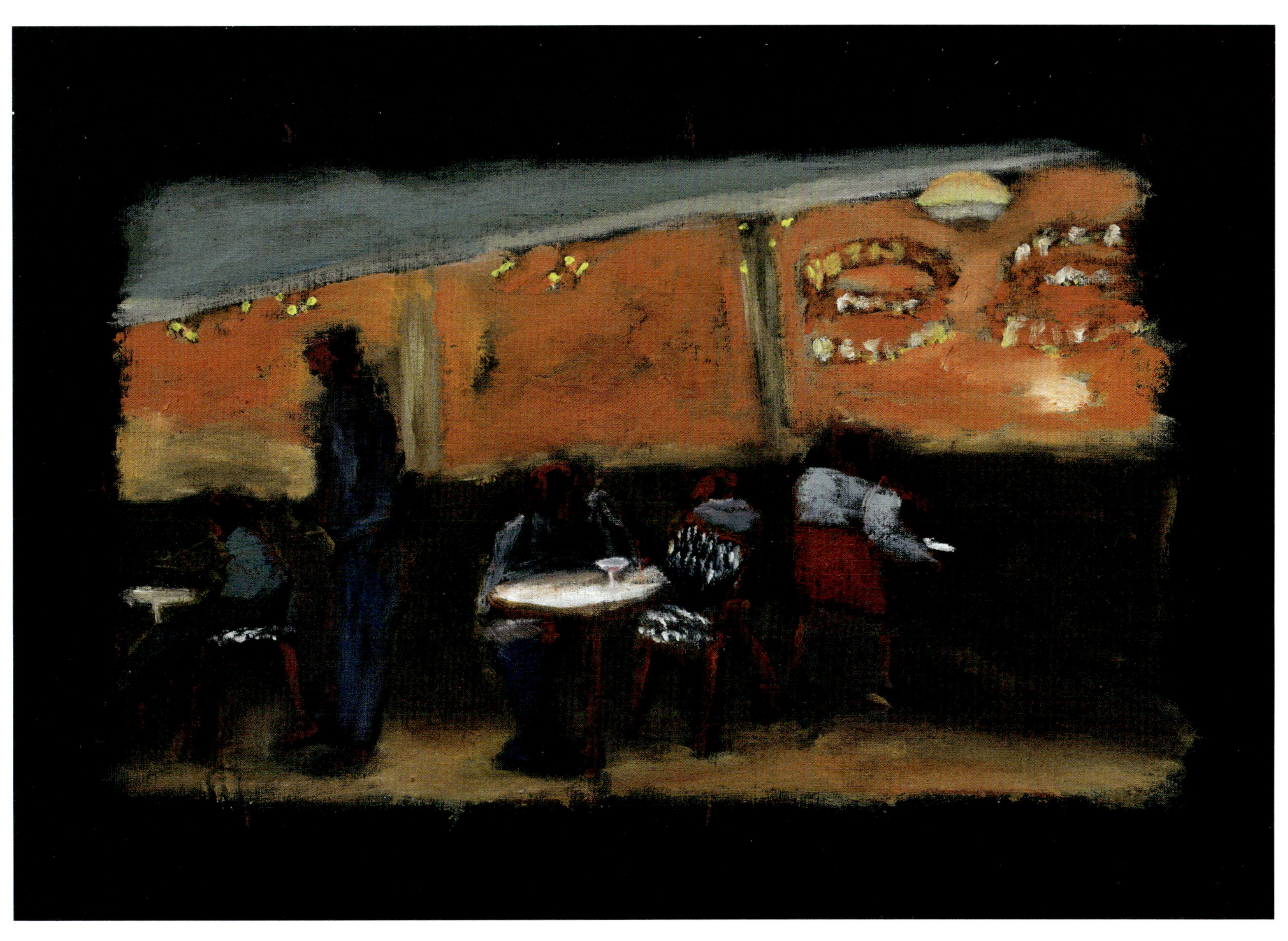



*Navy Days (Berlin)*, 2023

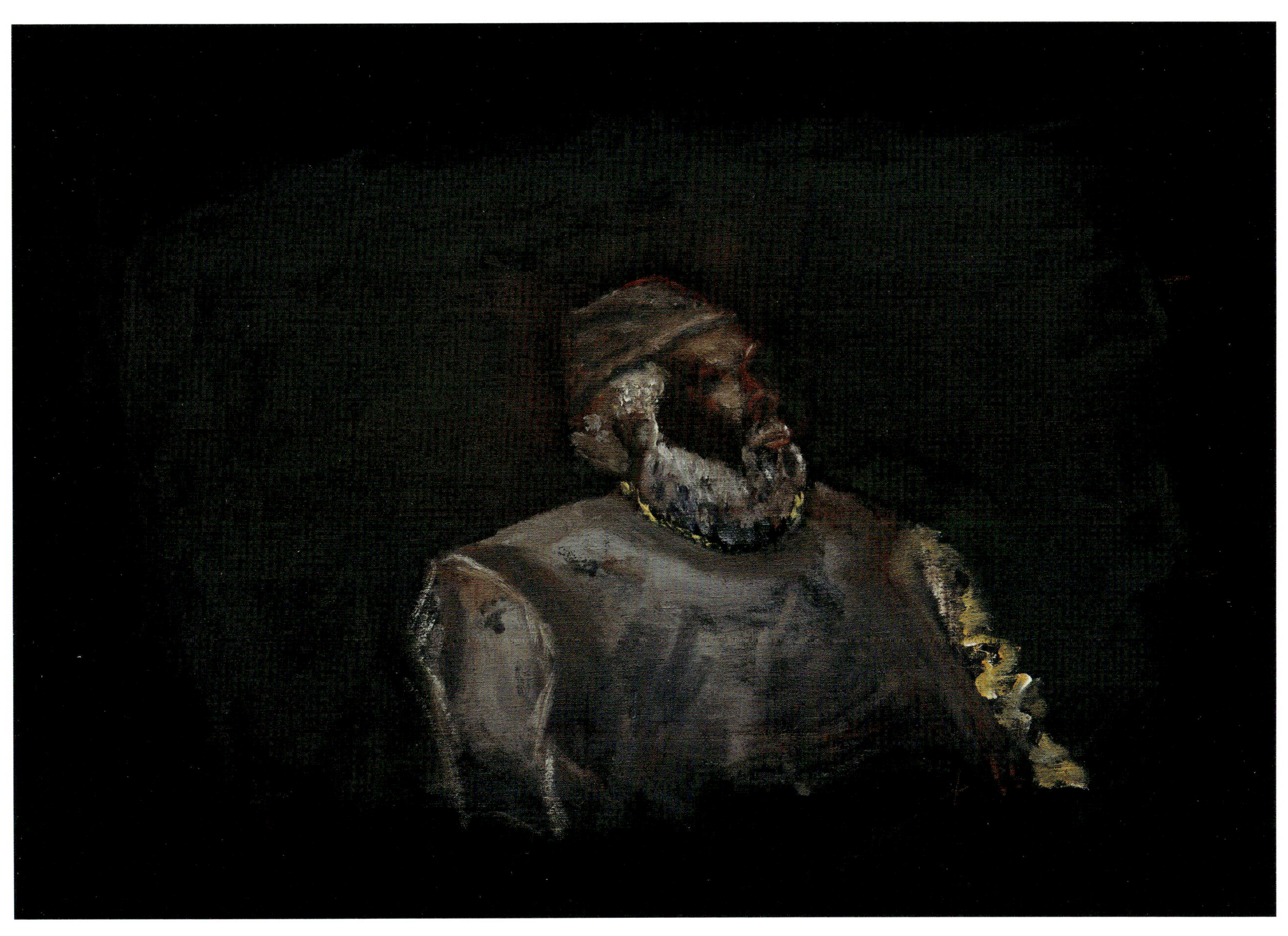



*Dangly Nerve (Berlin)*, 2023

# Copenhagen

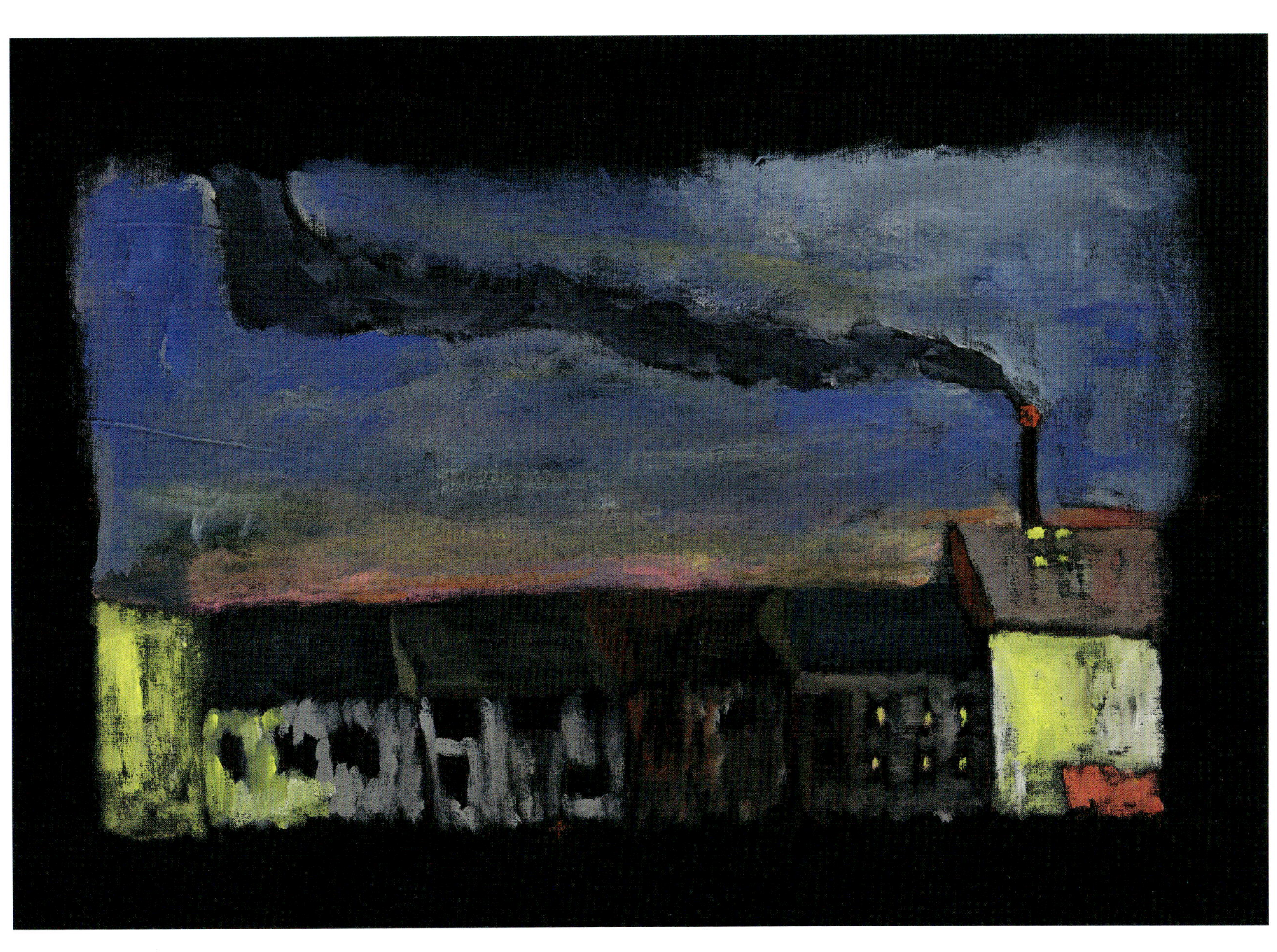

*Runa's Way (Copenhagen)*, 2023

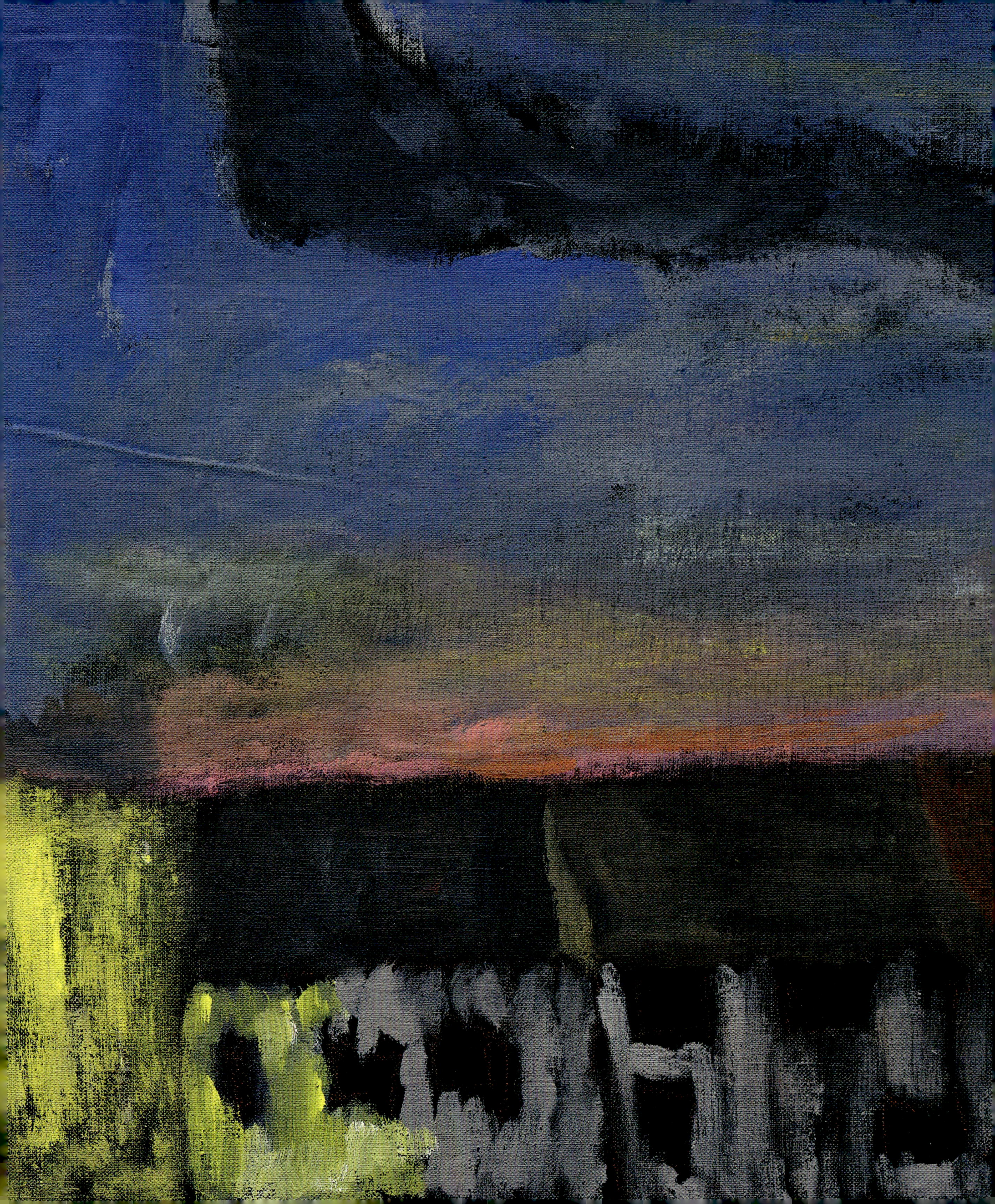

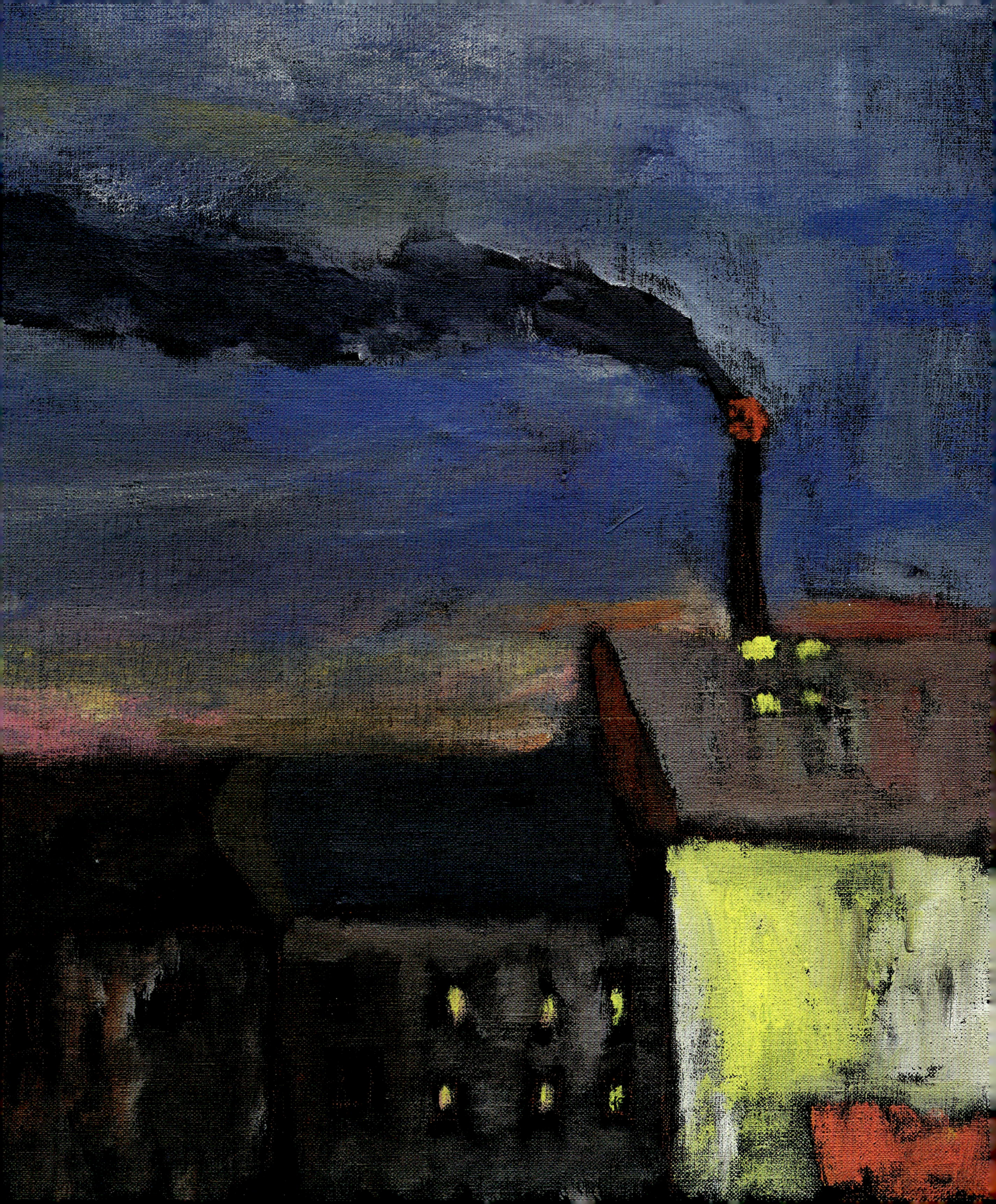

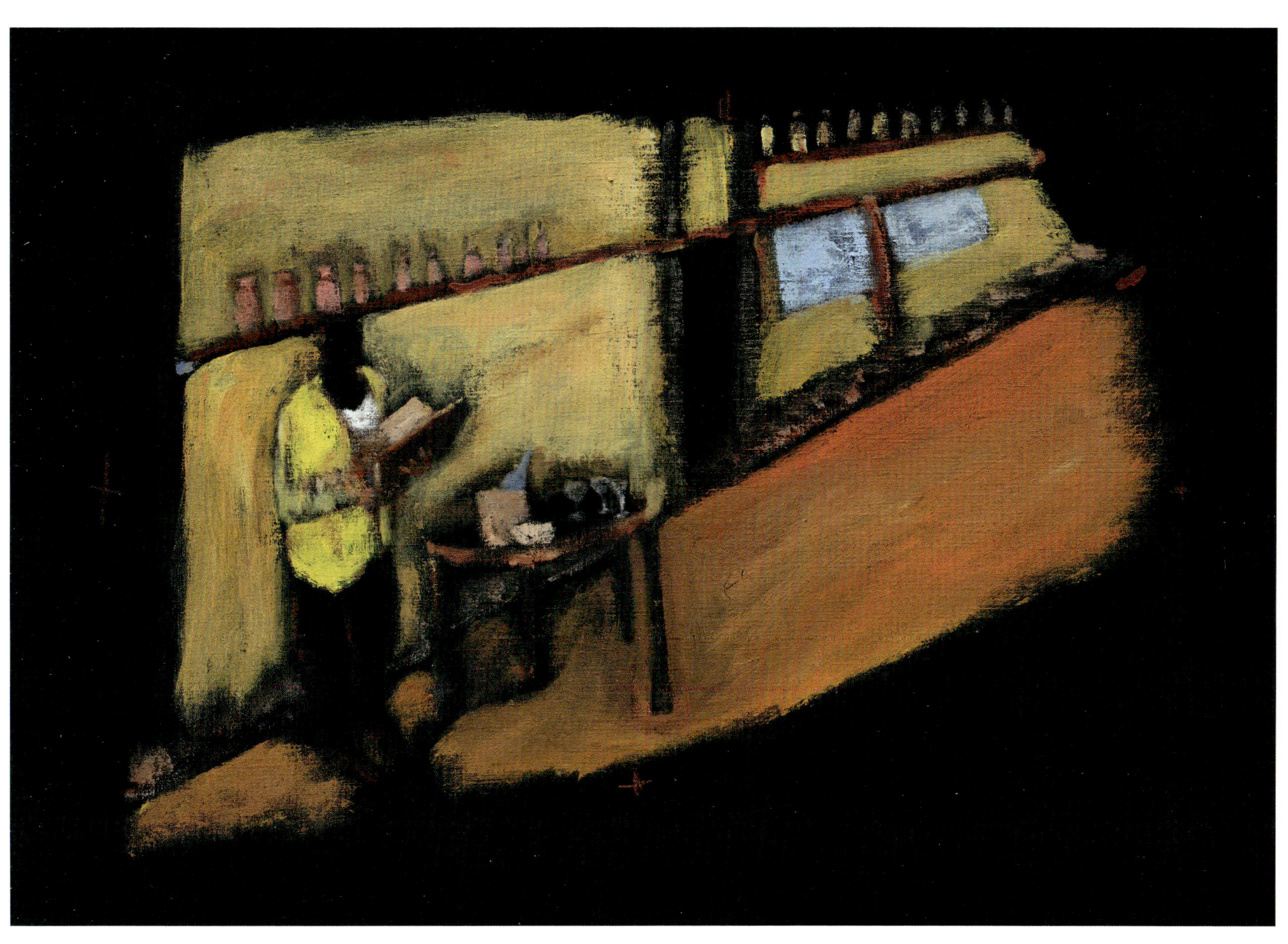

*Grand Consumption (Copenhagen)*, 2023

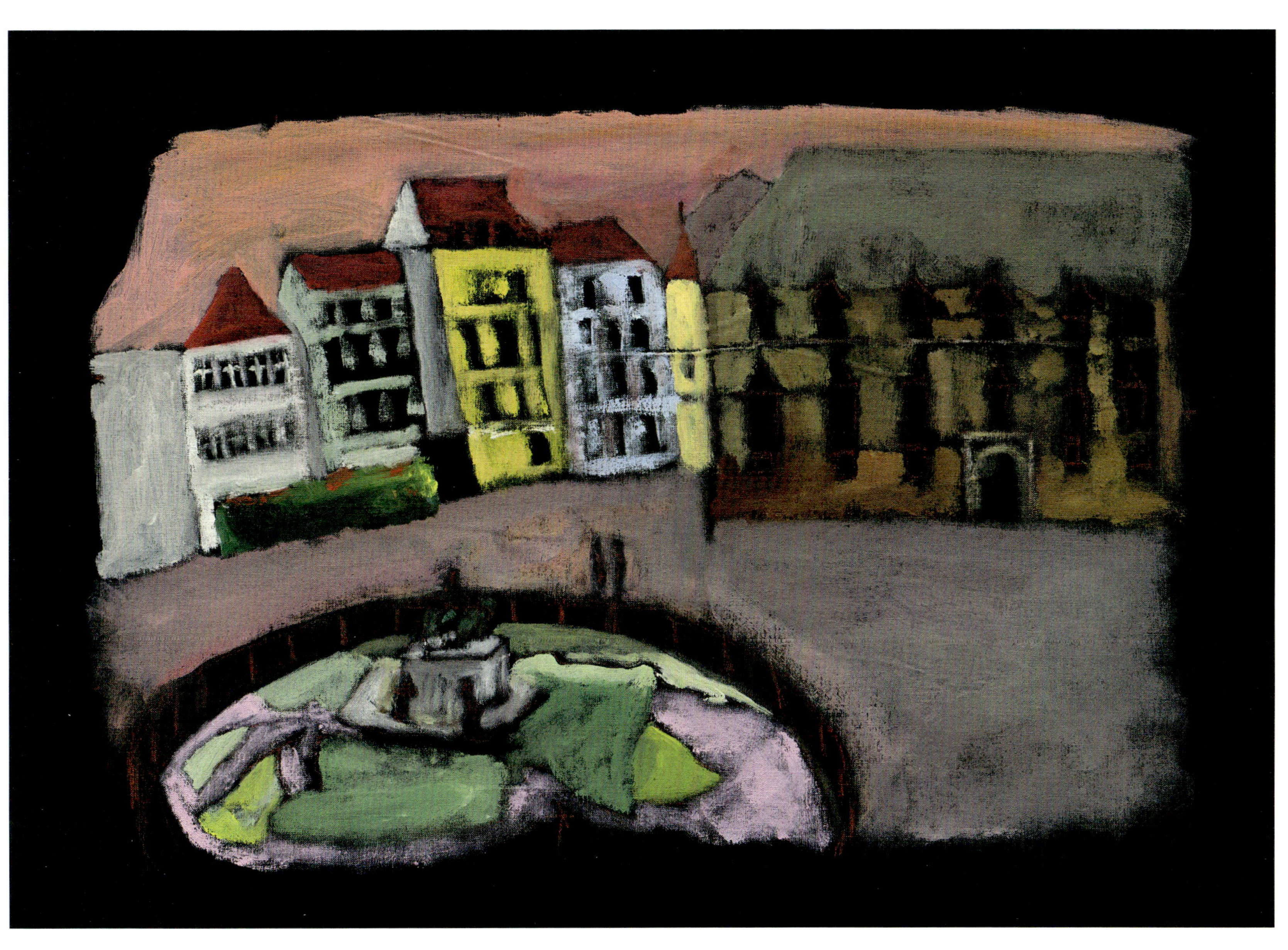

    *Three Churro's (Copenhagen)*, 2023

# Milan

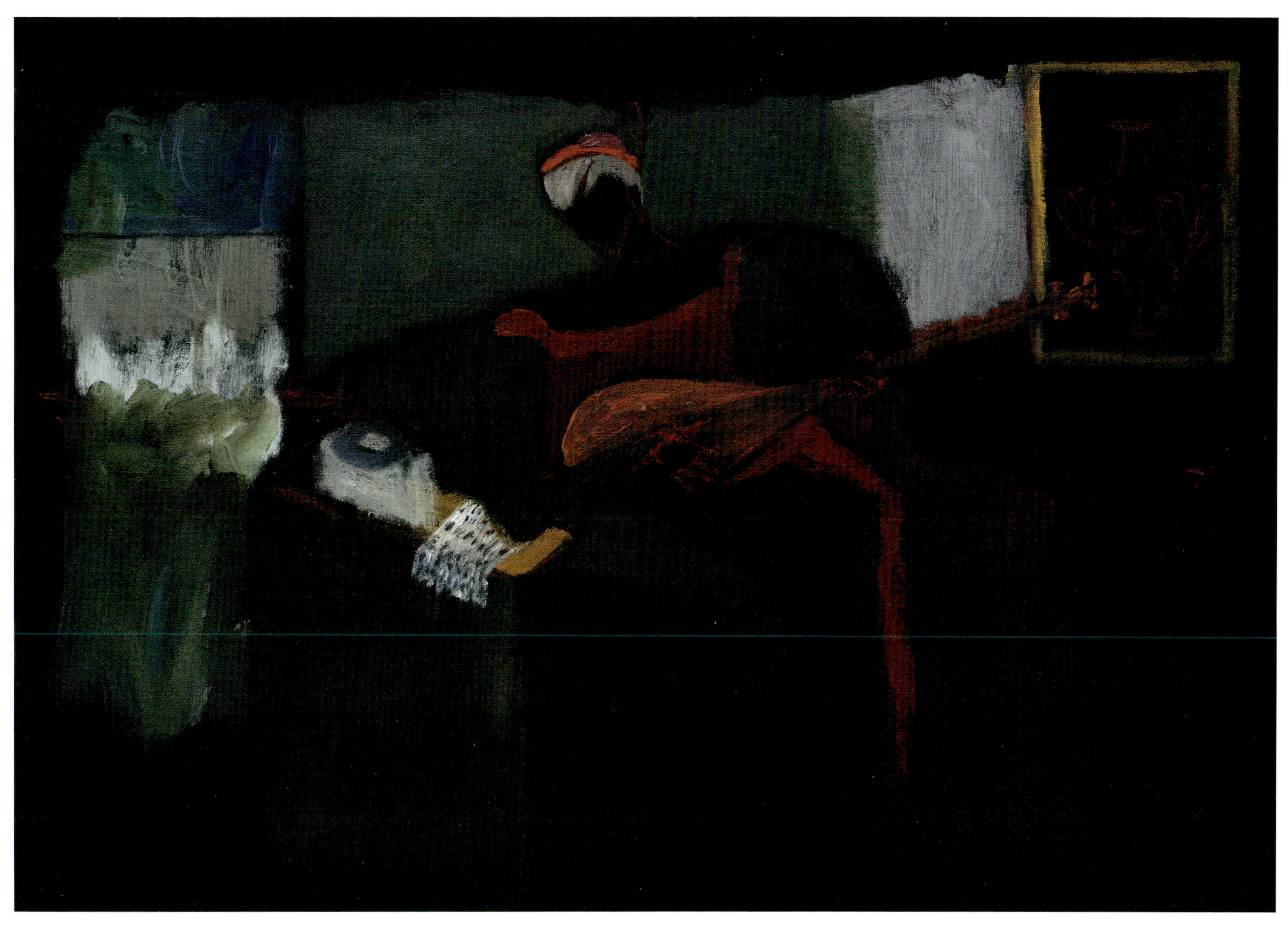



*Via Brera (Milan)*, 2023

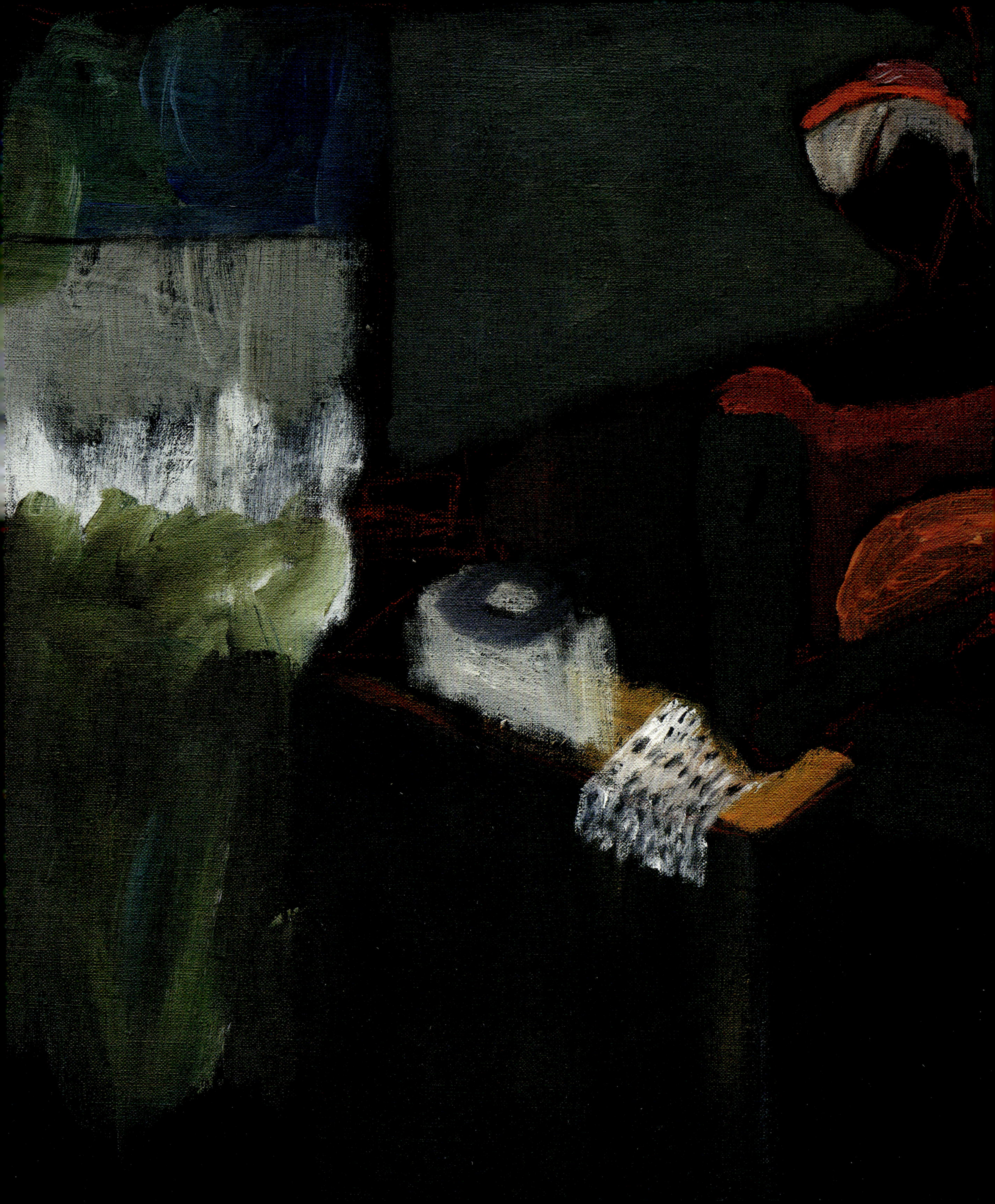

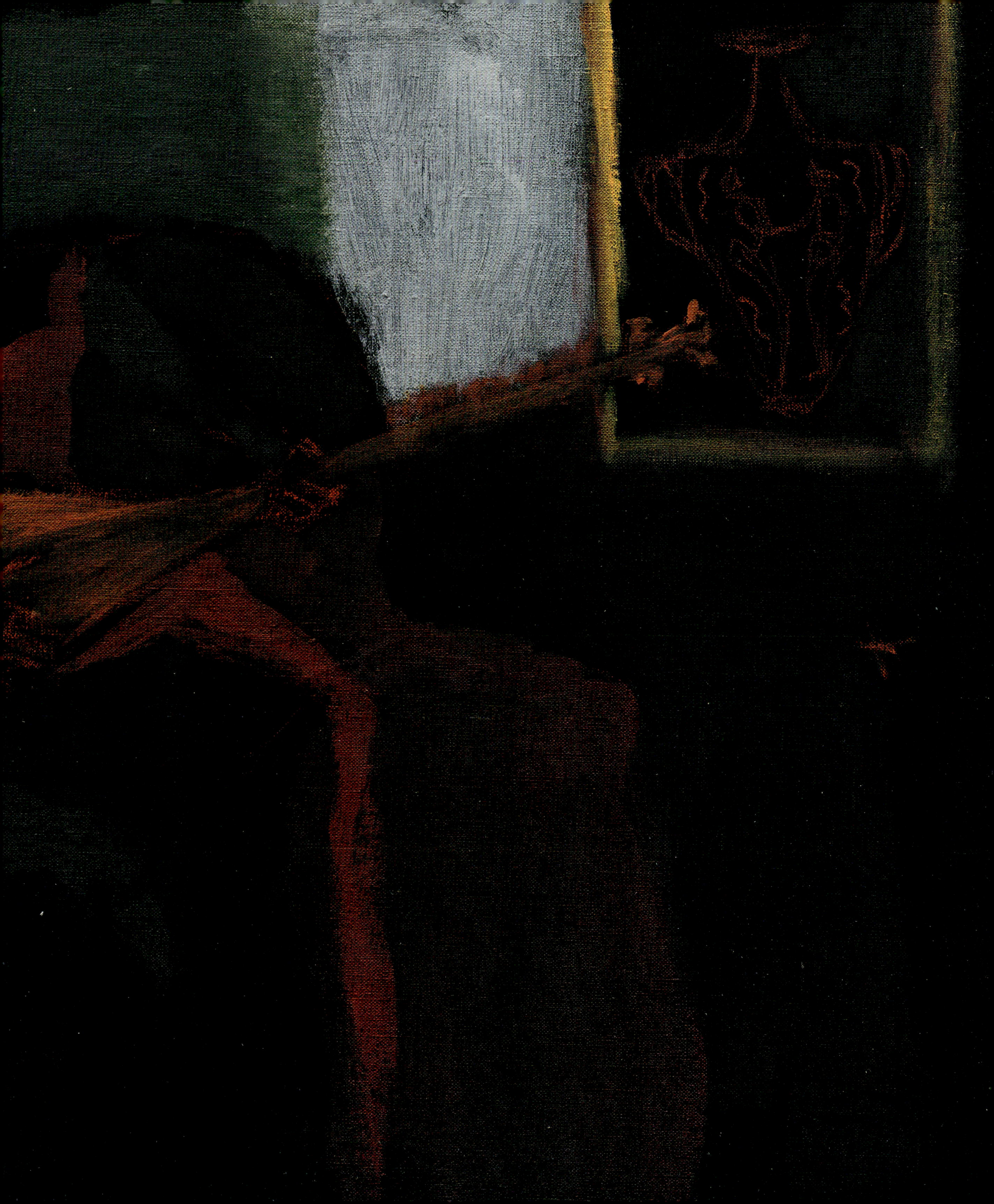

# Venice

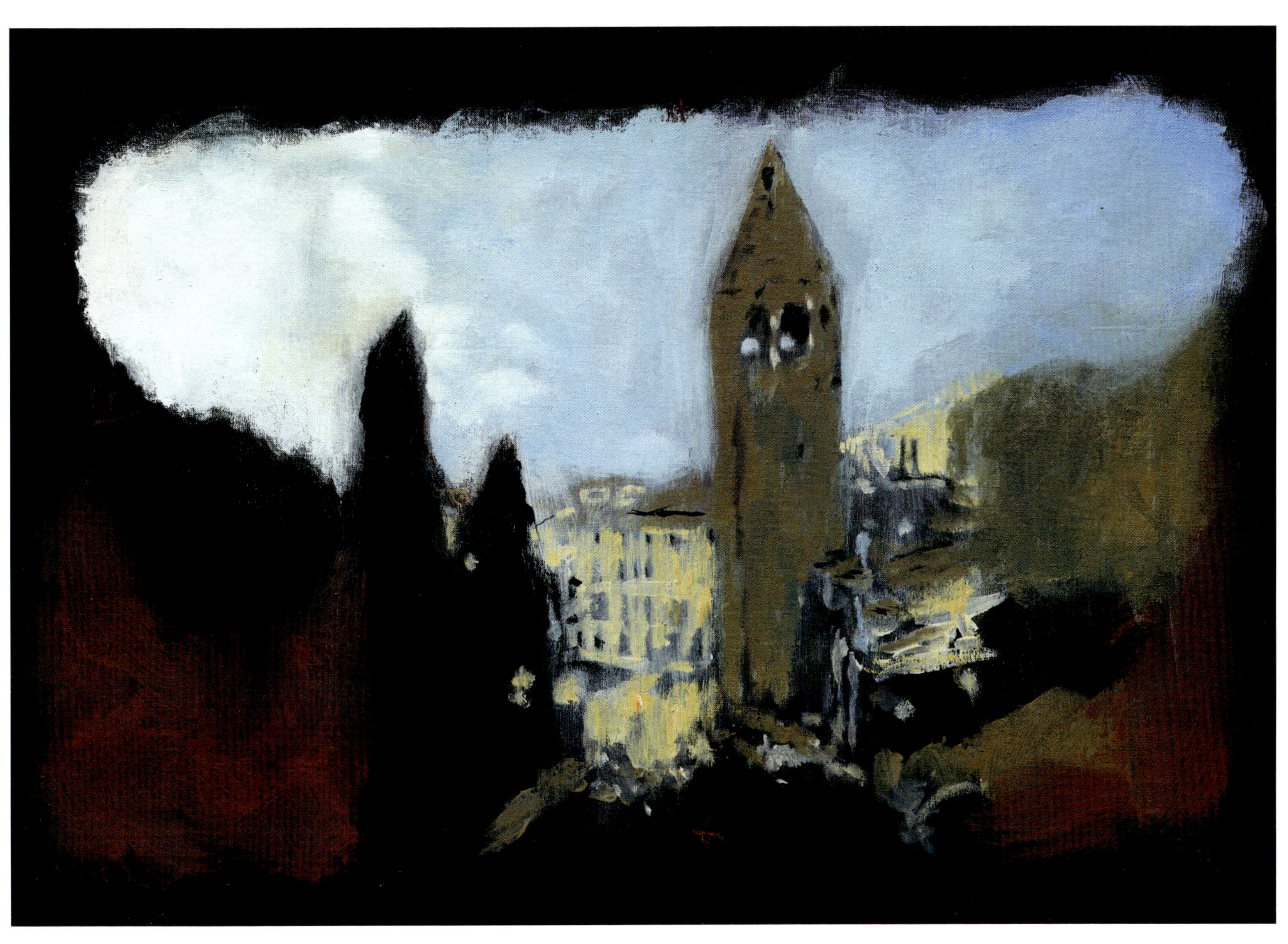



*Water Taxi (Venice)*, 2023

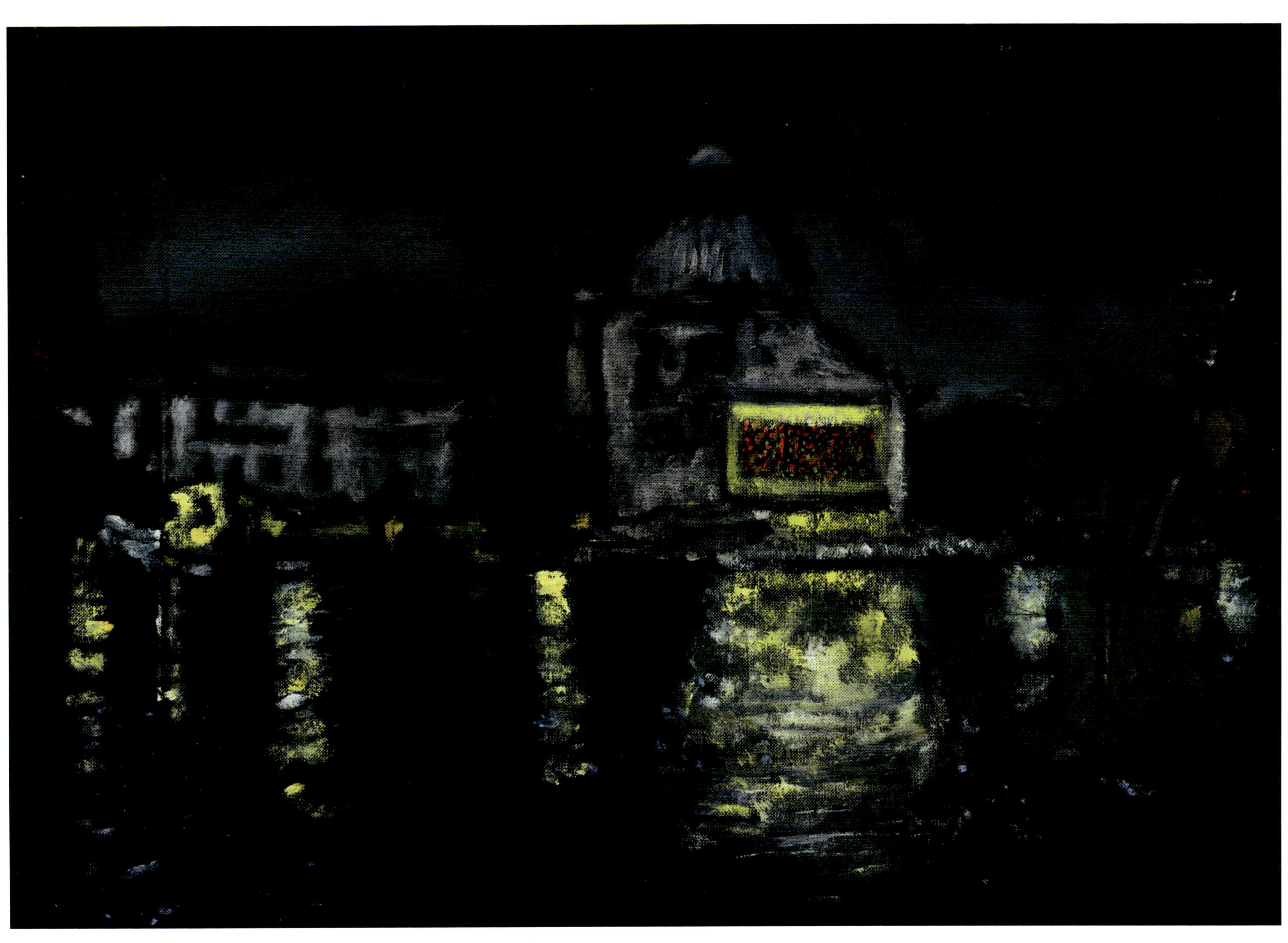



*Soft Scramble (Venice)*, 2023

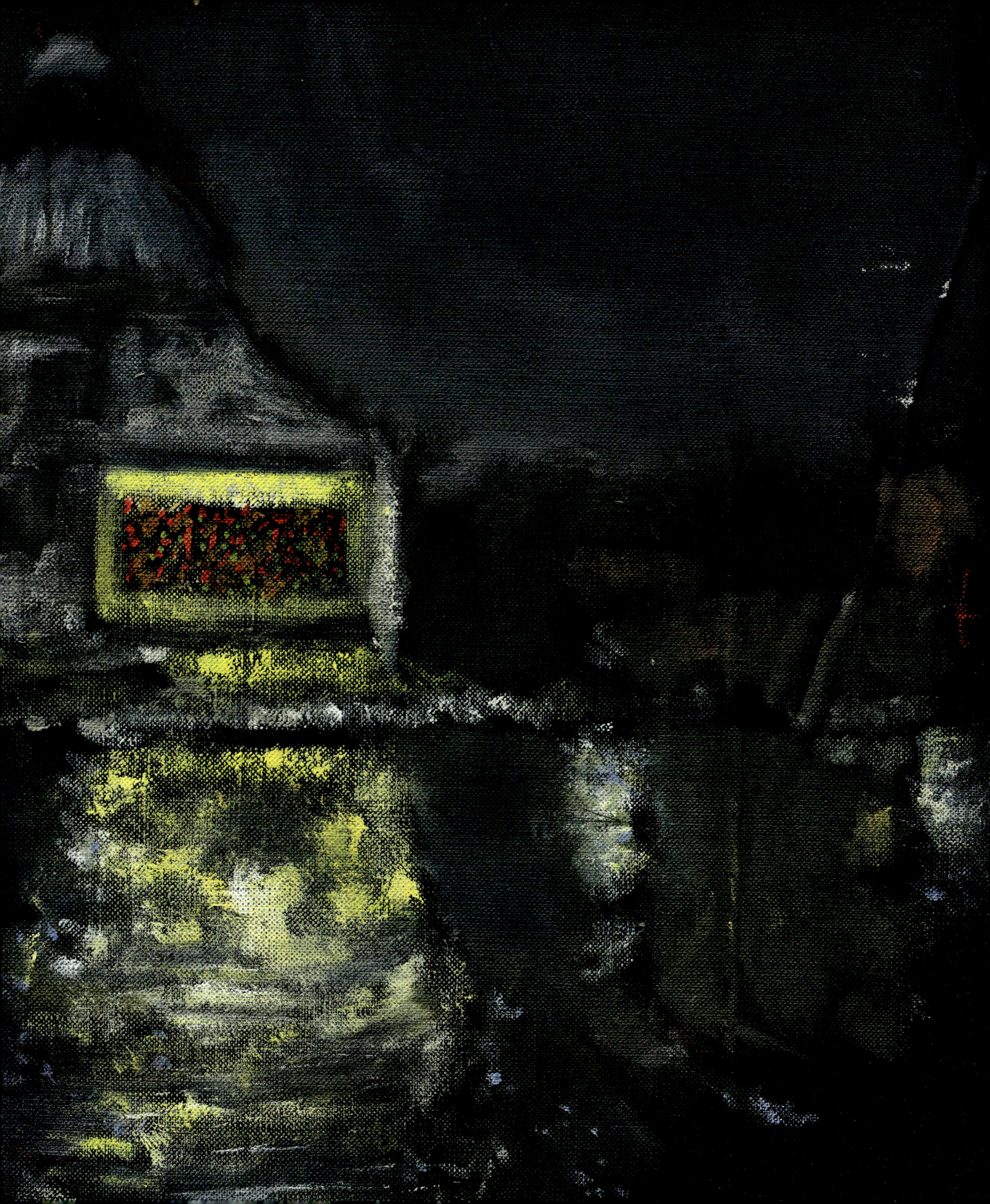

# Florence

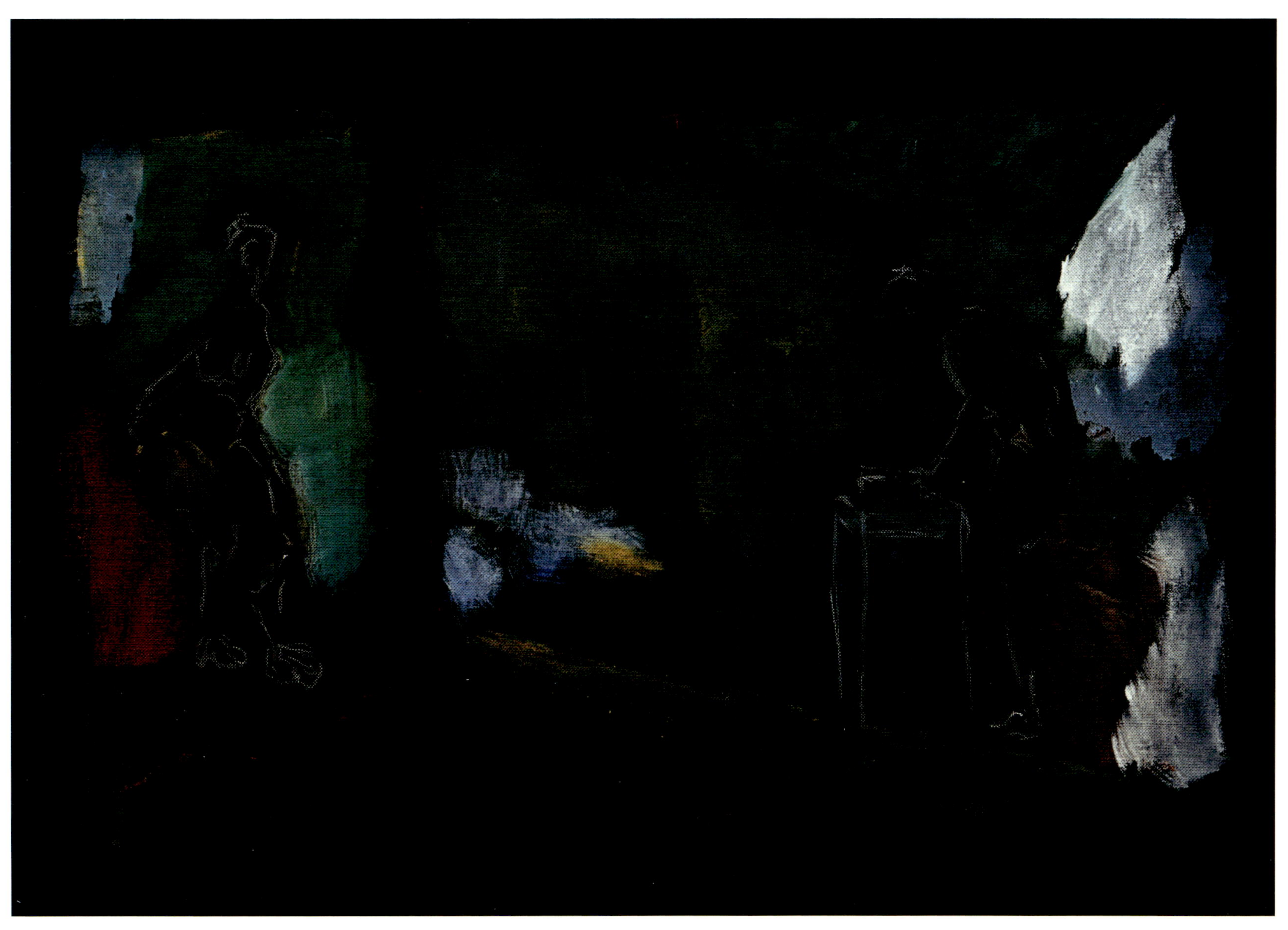



*Blue Ash (Florence)*, 2023

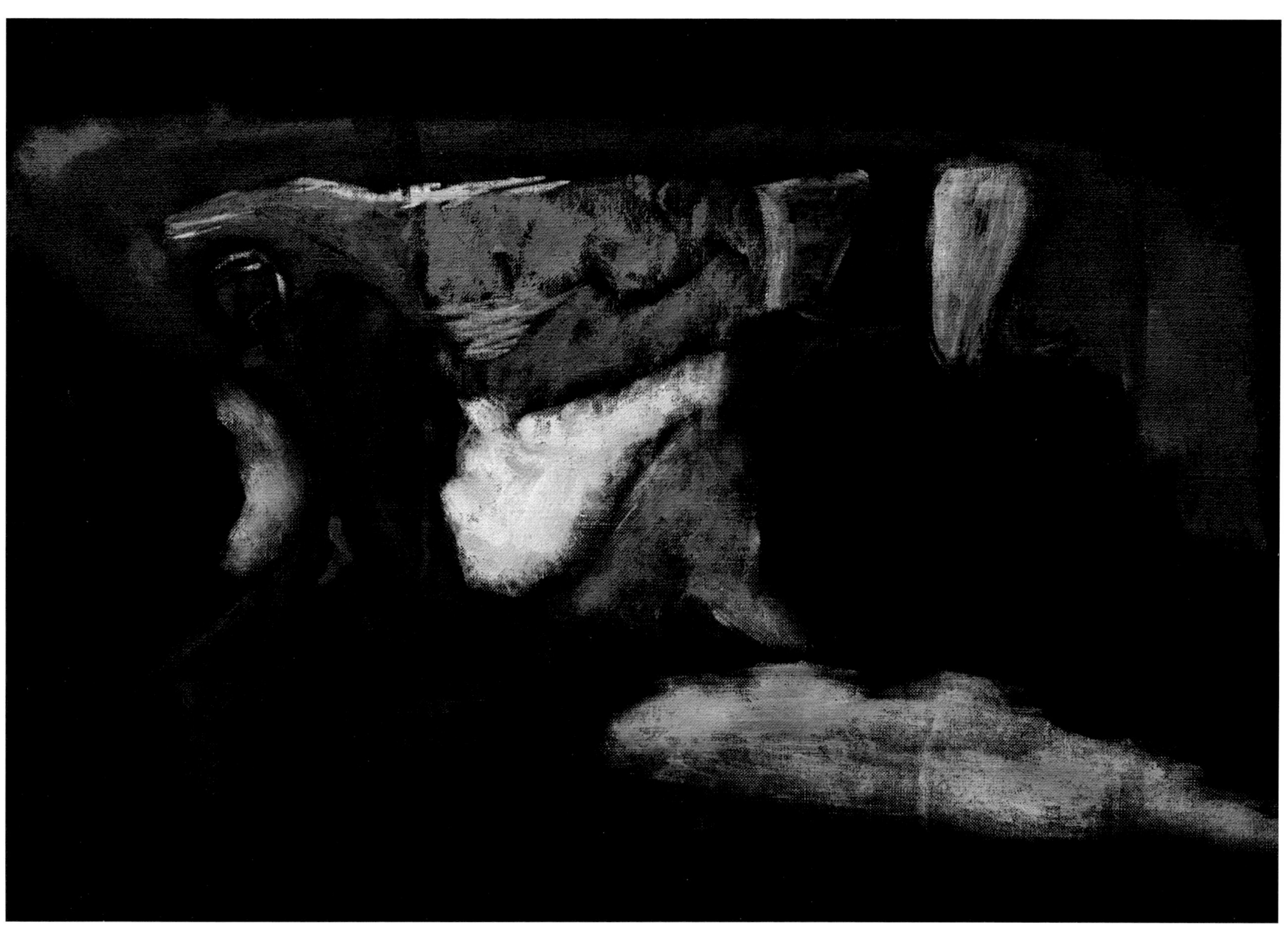

 *Root Cause (Florence)*, 2023

# Turin

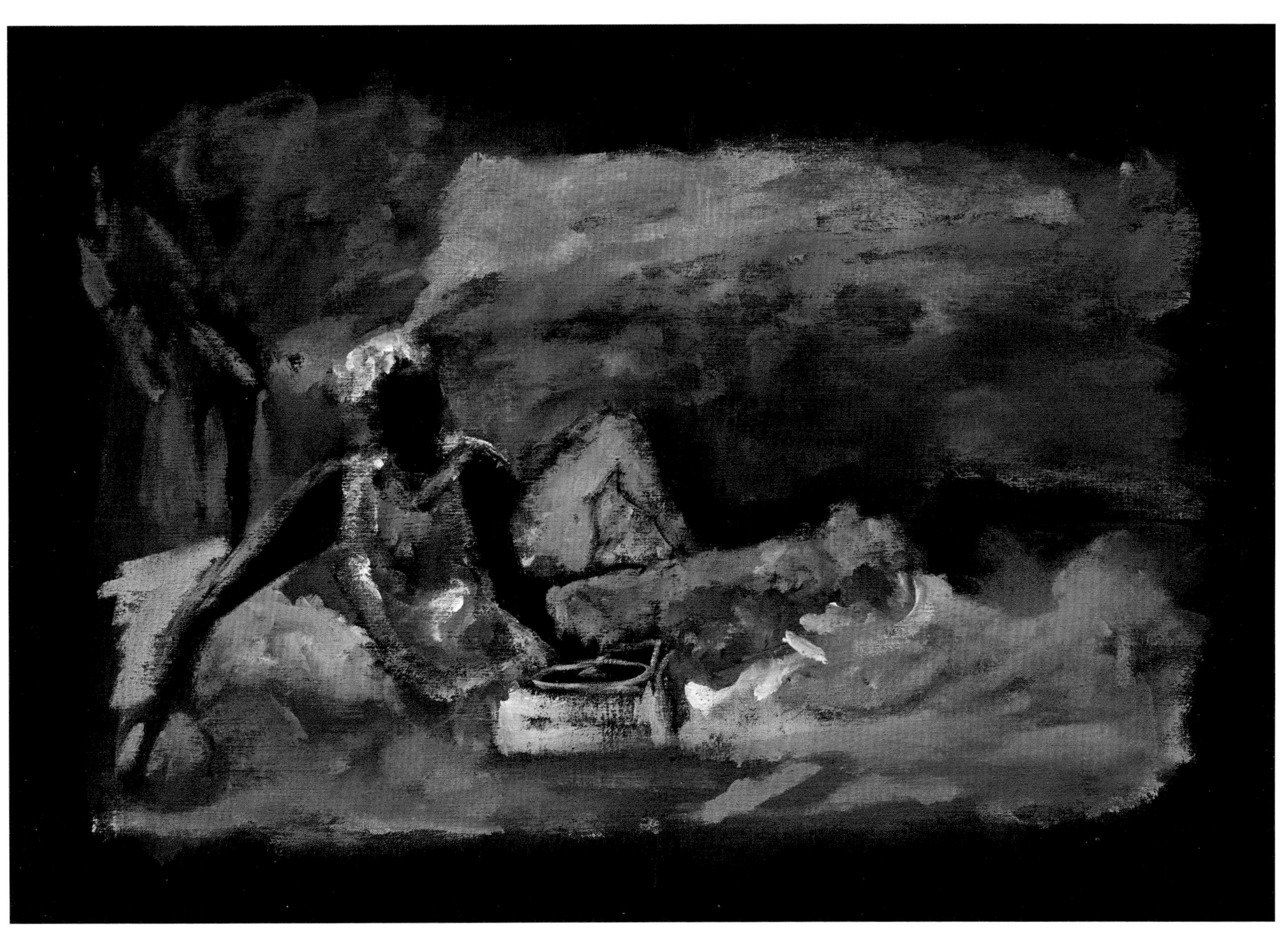



*Gaps In The Porcelain (Turin)*, 2023

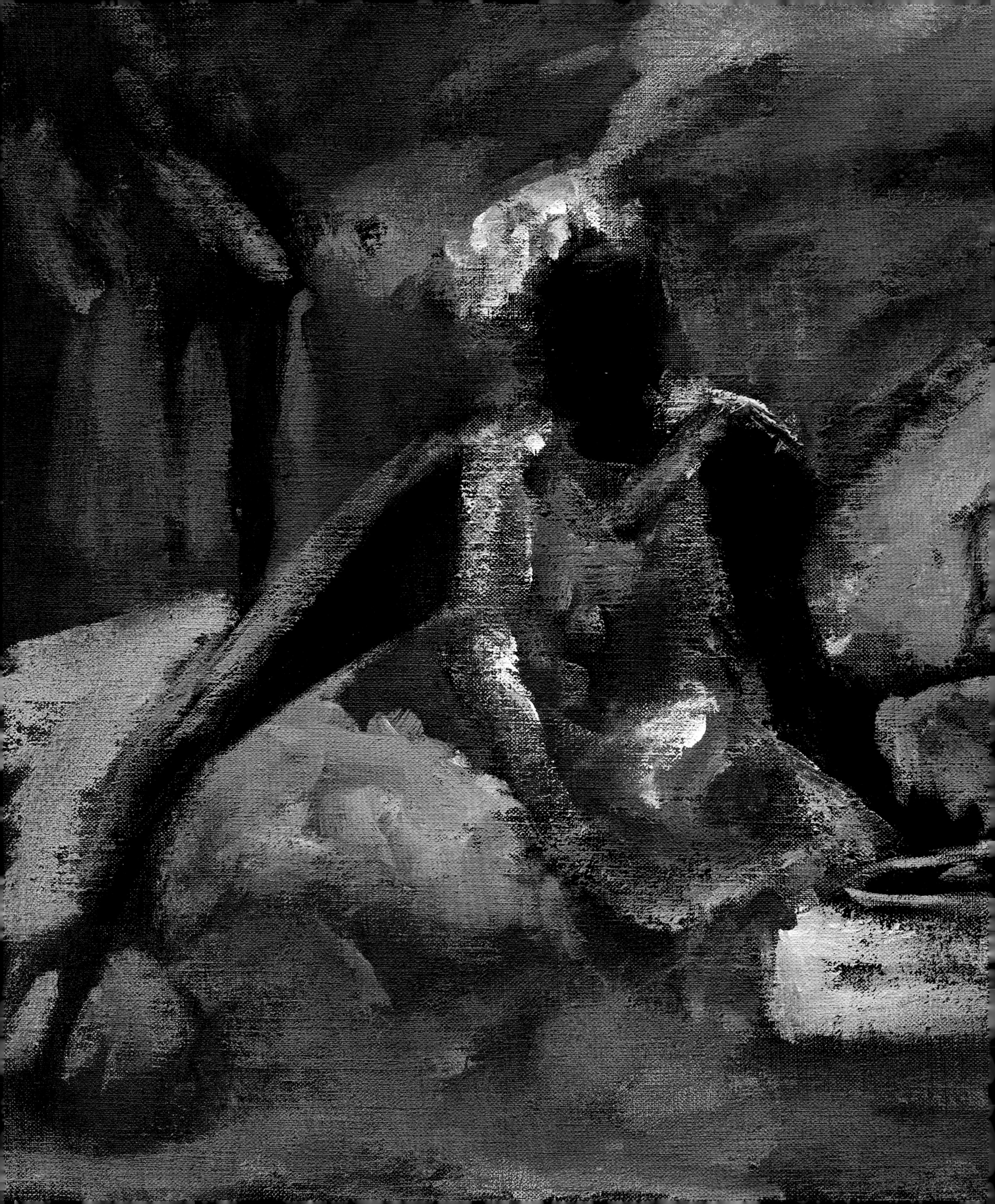

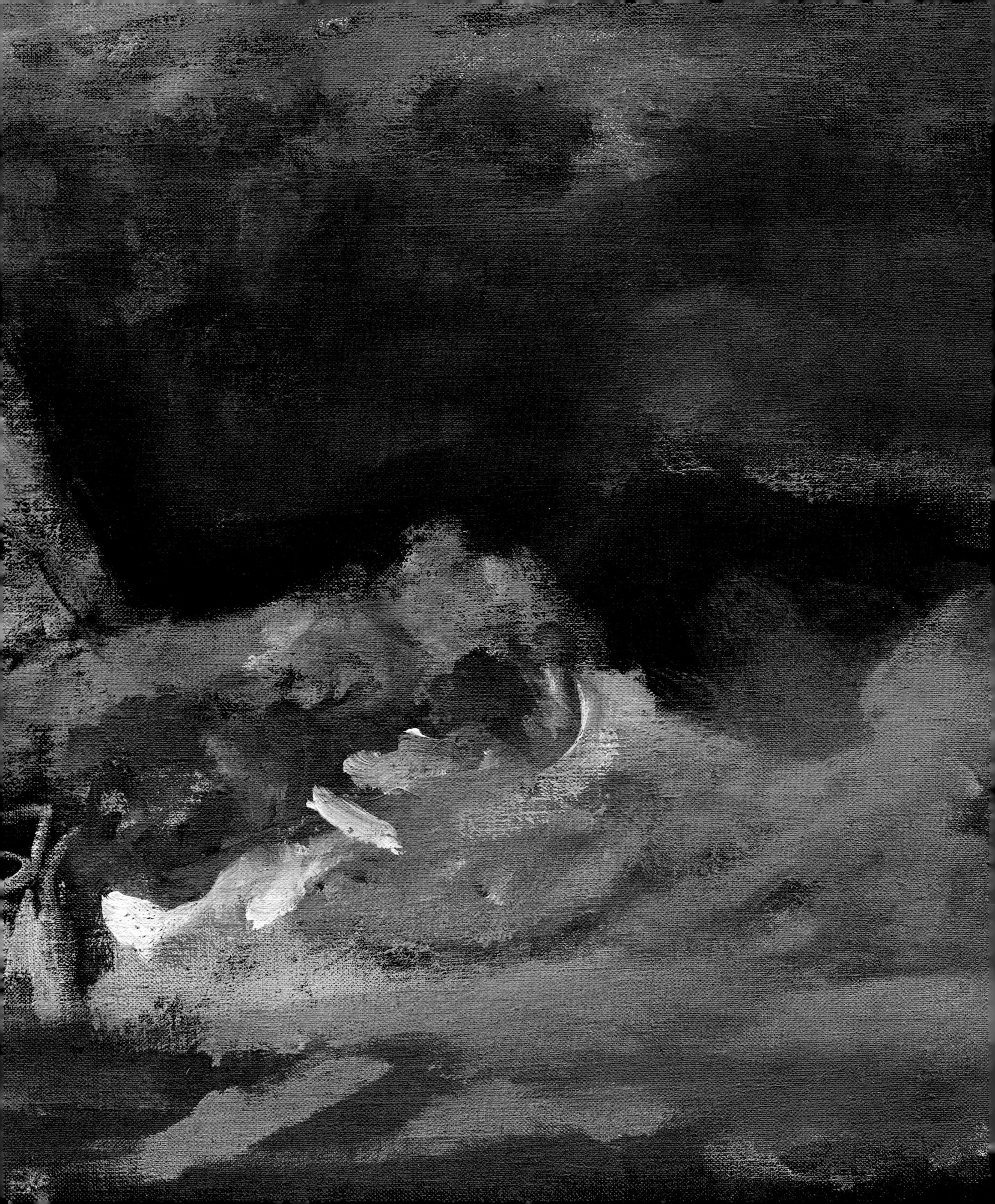

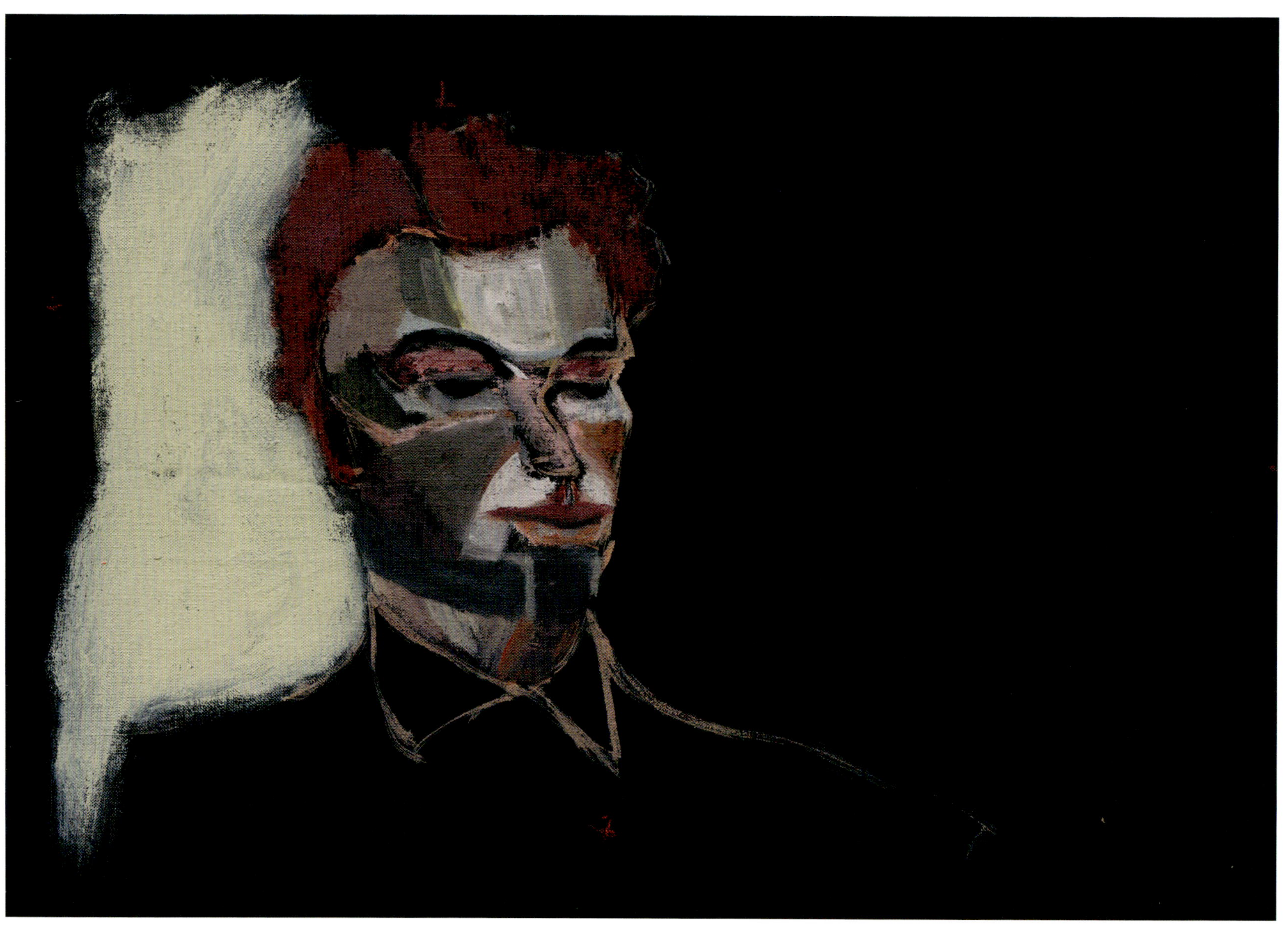



*Dhorta (Turin)*, 2023

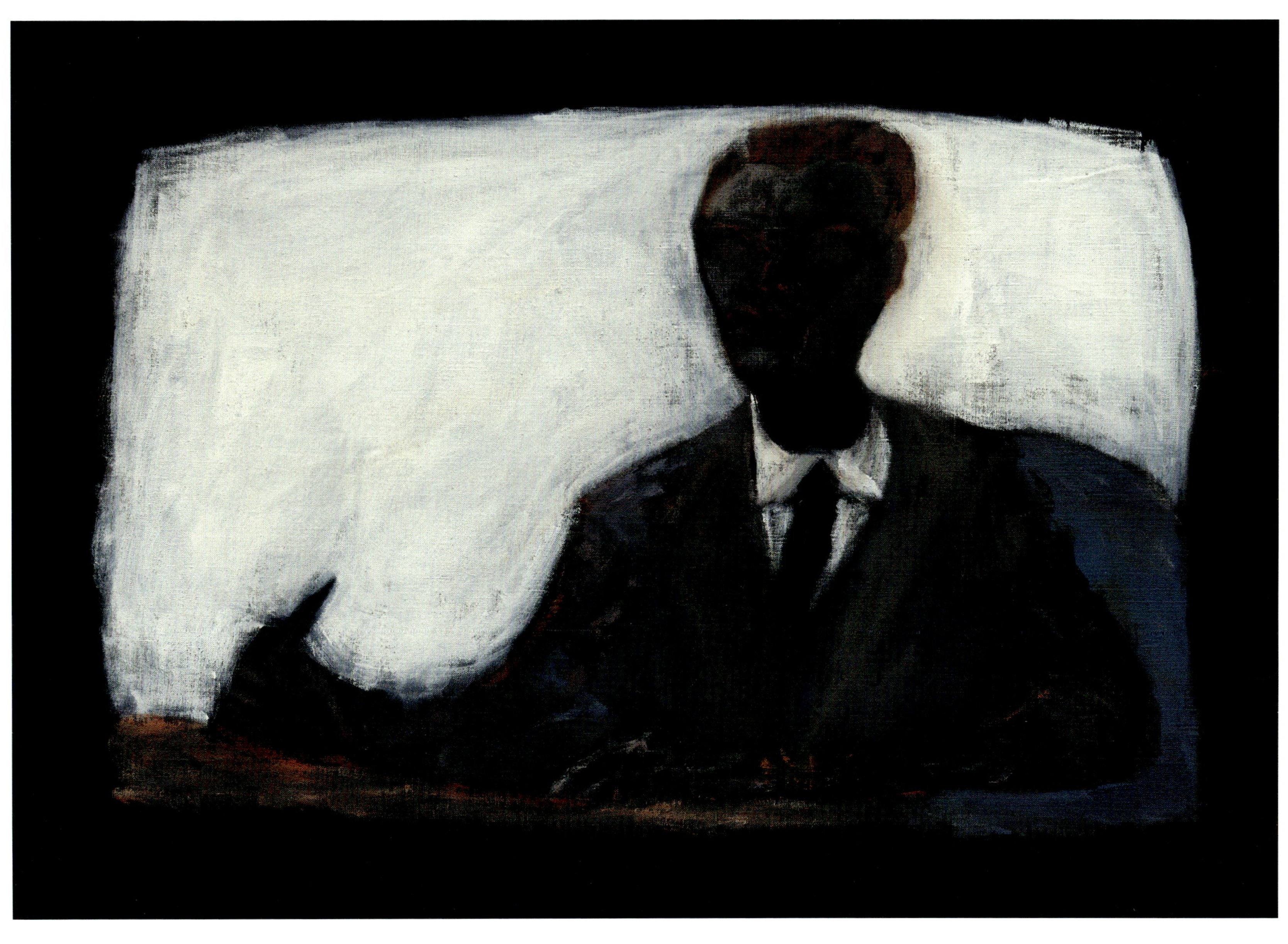

*Horatio Pudding (Turin)*, 2023

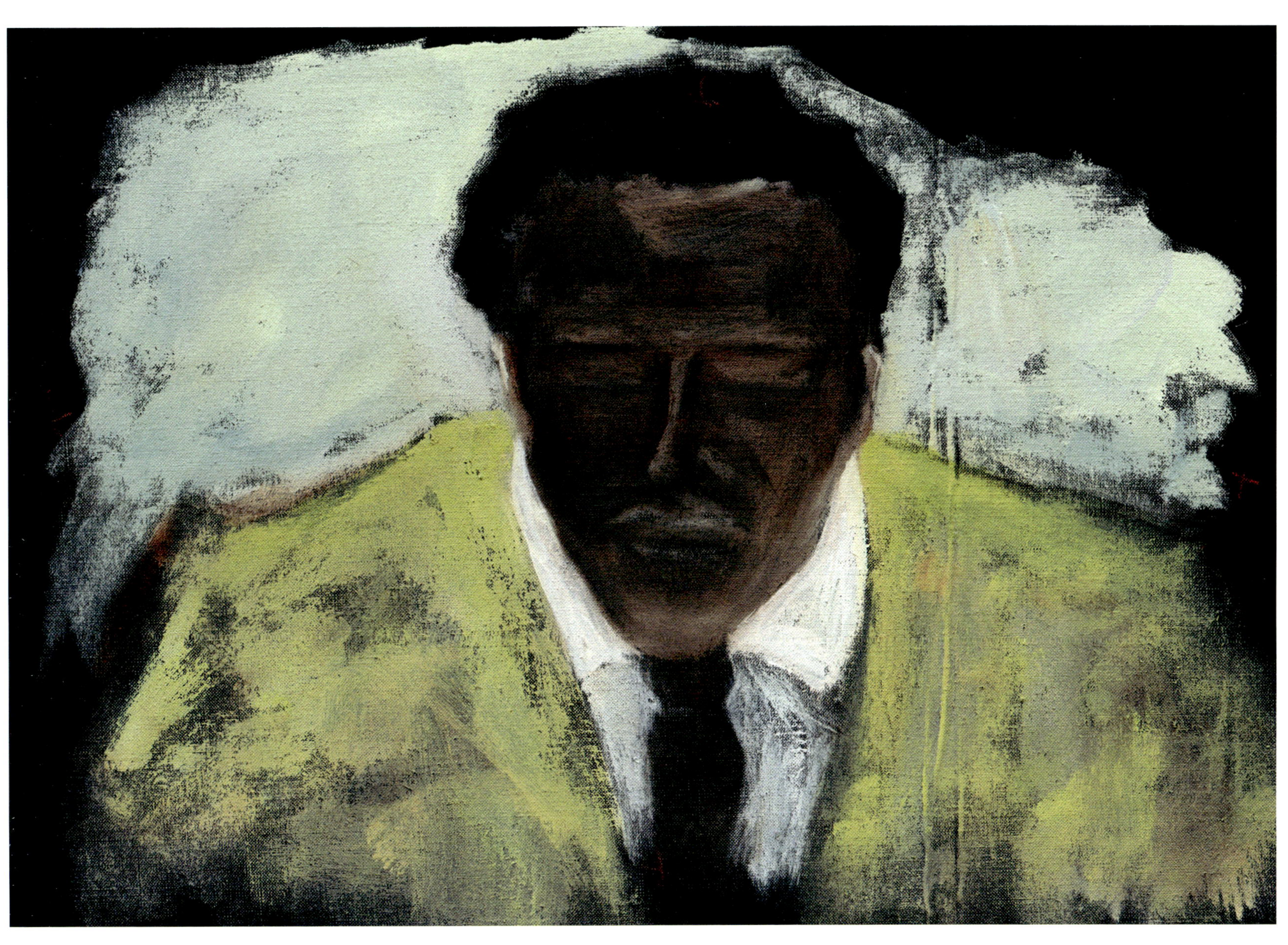



*Guiseppe Jaune (Turin)*, 2023

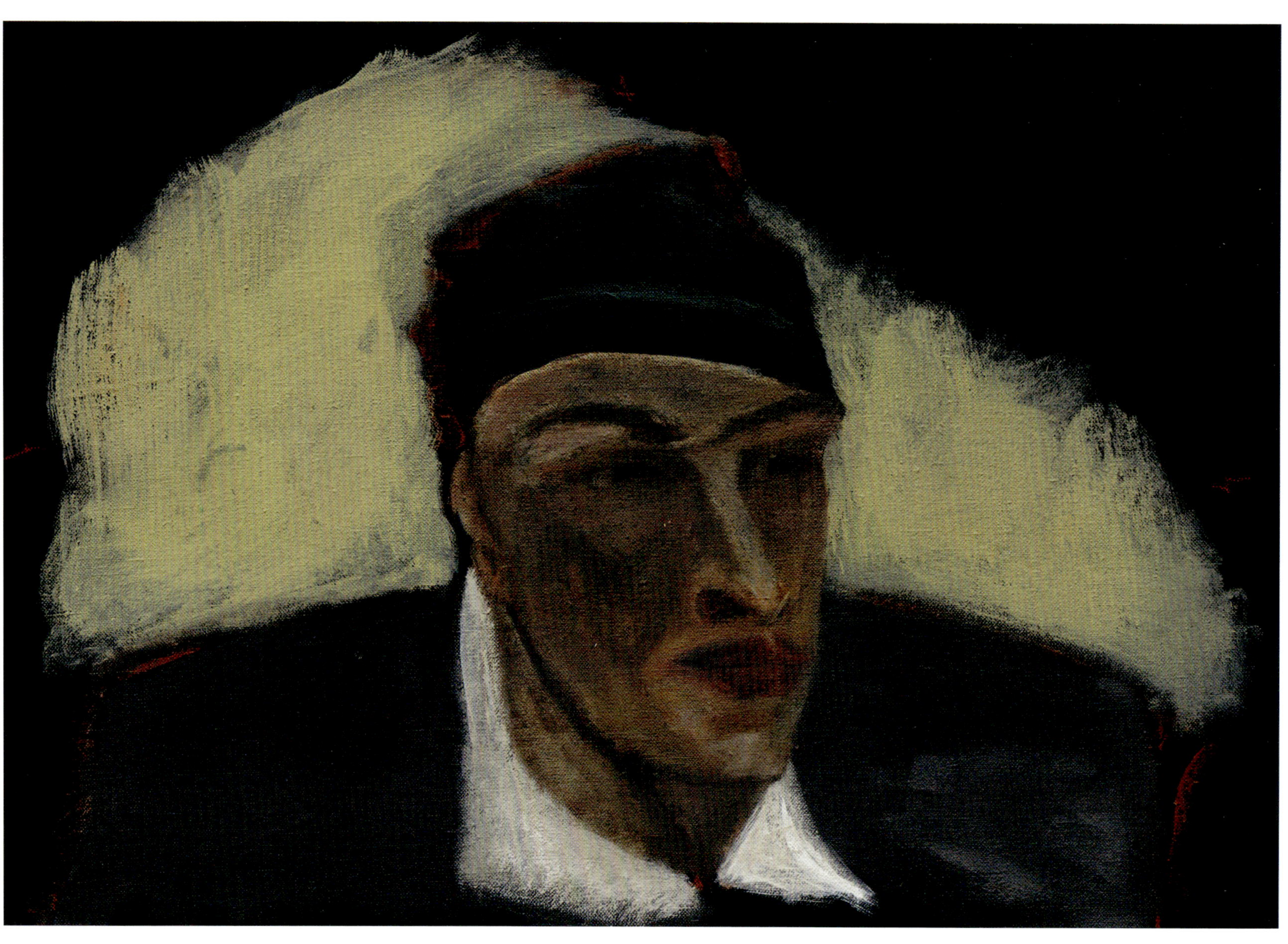



*Jericho Fit (Turin)*, 2023

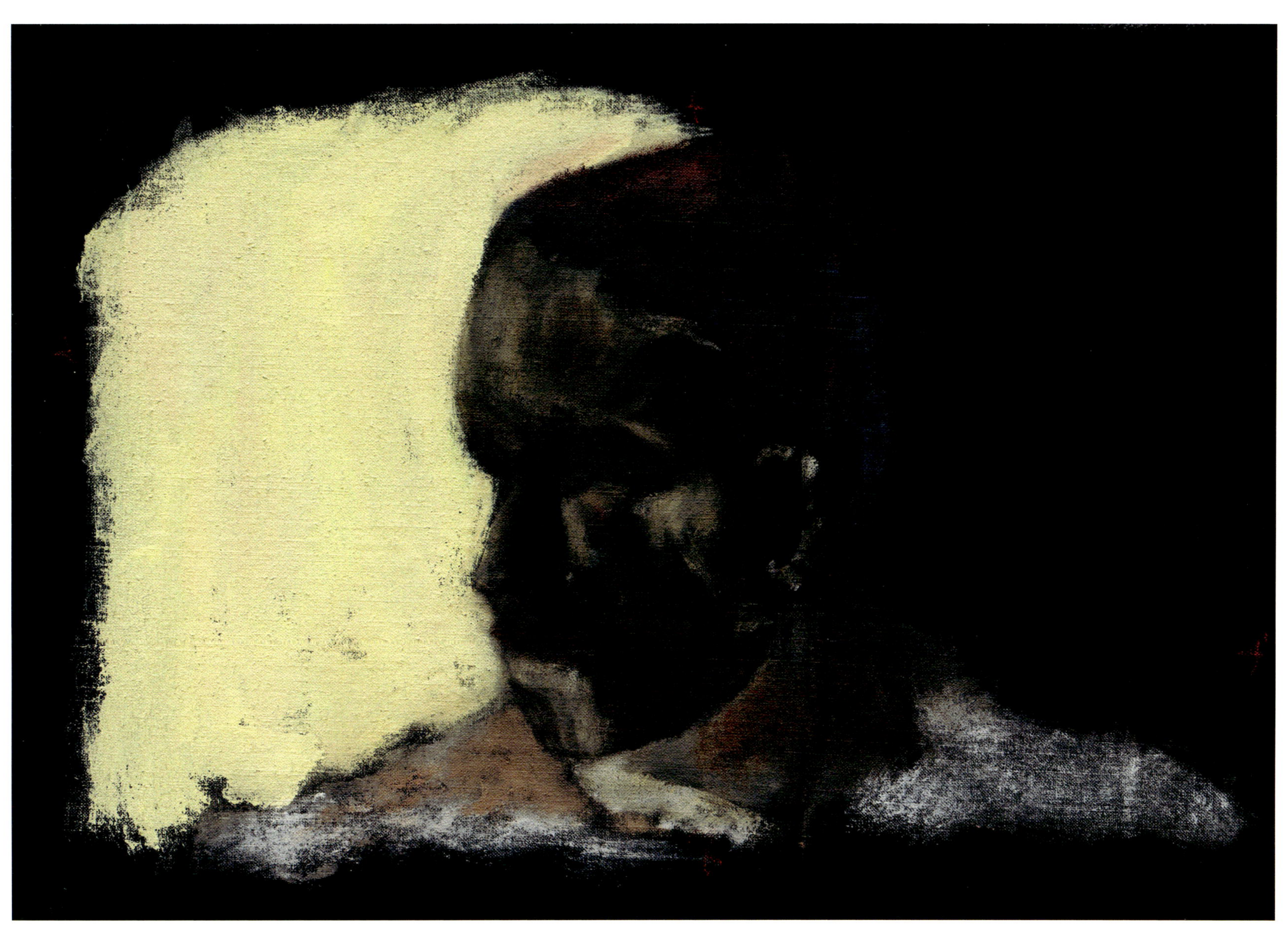



*Maria Peppers (Turin)*, 2023

Amsterdam

19–21
*Stepping Stone (Amsterdam)*, 2023
Acrylic and chalk pastel on linen
10 × 15 in. (25.4 × 38.1 cm)

23
*Thickly Settled (Amsterdam)*, 2023
Acrylic and chalk pastel on linen
10 × 15 in. (25.4 × 38.1 cm)

25
*Low Clearance (Amsterdam)*, 2023
Acrylic and chalk pastel on linen
10 × 15 in. (25.4 × 38.1 cm)


London

27
*Truffle Season (London)*, 2023
Acrylic and chalk pastel on linen
15 × 21 in. (38.1 × 53.3 cm)

28
*Dances Out Of Time (London)*, 2023
Acrylic and chalk pastel on linen
15 × 21 in. (38.1 × 53.3 cm)

29
*Level Ground (London)*, 2023
Acrylic and chalk pastel on linen
15 × 21 in. (38.1 × 53.3 cm)

31
*Coursed Out (London)*, 2023
Acrylic and chalk pastel on linen
15 × 21 in. (38.1 × 53.3 cm)

Paris

33–35
*Golden Triangle (Paris)*, 2023
Acrylic and chalk pastel on linen
15 × 21 in. (38.1 × 53.3 cm)

37–39
*Triomphe (Paris)*, 2023
Acrylic and chalk pastel on linen
15 × 21 in. (38.1 × 53.3 cm)

40
*Single Ticket (Paris)*, 2023
Acrylic and chalk pastel on linen
15 × 21 in. (38.1 × 53.3 cm)

41
*Signature (Paris)*, 2023
Acrylic and chalk pastel on linen
15 × 21 in. (38.1 × 53.3 cm)

43
*The Duet (Paris)*, 2023
Acrylic and chalk pastel on linen
15 × 21 in. (38.1 × 53.3 cm)

45
*Wordless (Paris)*, 2023
Acrylic and chalk pastel on linen
15 × 21 in. (38.1 × 53.3 cm)

46
*Rosewood (Paris)*, 2023
Acrylic on linen
15 × 21 in. (38.1 × 53.3 cm)

47
*Calm Crillon (Paris)*, 2023
Acrylic and chalk pastel on linen
15 × 21 in. (38.1 × 53.3 cm)

49
*Impetus For The Gala (Paris)*, 2023
Acrylic and chalk pastel on linen
15 × 21 in. (38.1 × 53.3 cm)

Berlin

51
*Navy Days (Berlin)*, 2023
Acrylic and chalk pastel on linen
15 × 21 in. (38.1 × 53.3 cm)

53
*Dangly Nerve (Berlin)*, 2023
Acrylic and chalk pastel on linen
15 × 21 in. (38.1 × 53.3 cm)

Copenhagen

55–57
*Runa's Way (Copenhagen)*, 2023
Acrylic and chalk pastel on linen
15 × 21 in. (38.1 × 53.3 cm)

59
*Grand Consumption (Copenhagen)*, 2023
Acrylic and chalk pastel on linen
15 × 21 in. (38.1 × 53.3 cm)

61
*Three Churro's (Copenhagen)*, 2023
Acrylic and chalk pastel on linen
15 × 21 in. (38.1 × 53.3 cm)

Milan

63–65
*Via Brera (Milan)*, 2023
Acrylic and chalk pastel on linen
15 × 21 in. (38.1 × 53.3 cm)

Venice

67
*Water Taxi (Venice)*, 2023
Acrylic and chalk pastel on linen
15 × 21 in. (38.1 × 53.3 cm)

69–71
*Soft Scramble (Venice)*, 2023
Acrylic and chalk pastel on linen
15 × 21 in. (38.1 × 53.3 cm)

Florence

73
*Blue Ash (Florence)*, 2023
Acrylic and chalk pastel on linen
15 × 21 in. (38.1 × 53.3 cm)

75
*Root Cause (Florence)*, 2023
Acrylic and chalk pastel on linen
15 × 21 in. (38.1 × 53.3 cm)

Turin

77–79
*Gaps In The Porcelain (Turin)*, 2023
Acrylic and chalk pastel on linen
15 × 21 in. (38.1 × 53.3 cm)

80
*Dhorta (Turin)*, 2023
Acrylic and chalk pastel on linen
15 × 21 in. (38.1 × 53.3 cm)

81
*Horatio Pudding (Turin)*, 2023
Acrylic and chalk pastel on linen
15 × 21 in. (38.1 × 53.3 cm)

83
*Guiseppe Jaune (Turin)*, 2023
Acrylic and chalk pastel on linen
15 × 21 in. (38.1 × 53.3 cm)

84
*Jericho Fit (Turin)*, 2023
Acrylic and chalk pastel on linen
15 × 21 in. (38.1 × 53.3 cm)

85
*Maria Peppers (Turin)*, 2023
Acrylic and chalk pastel on linen
15 × 21 in. (38.1 × 53.3 cm)

This book is published in conjunction with

Reggie Burrows Hodges
*Authorities of Reason*

Karma
7351 Santa Monica Boulevard
Los Angeles
January 11–February 13, 2025